BEYOND THE BODY!
DEVELOPING INNER BEAUTY

Edited by Linda Ellis Eastman

Professional Woman Publishing
Prospect, Kentucky

BEYOND THE BODY! DEVELOPING INNER BEAUTY
Copyright © 2007 by Linda Ellis Eastman
All rights reserved.

Published by:
Professional Woman Publishing
Post Office Box 333
Prospect, KY 40059
(502) 228-0906
http://www.prowoman.net

Please contact the publisher for quantity discounts.

ISBN 13: 978-0-9799711-1-2
ISBN 10: 0-9799711-1-x

Library of Congress Cataloging-In-Publication Data

Cover Design and Typography by:
Sential Design, LLC — www.sentialdesign.com

Printed in the United States of America

Dedicated to Linda Riser who was simply beautiful within.

TABLE OF CONTENTS

Introduction — ix
Linda Ellis Eastman

1. Mental Clutter — 3
Dr. Tammy McDonald

2. A Bill of Rights for the Assertive Woman — 17
Alice Maxin

3. Setting Personal Goals — 31
April Jones

4. The Art of Forgiveness — 43
Karen Deslandes

5. Embracing Fear — 55
Riki Lovejoy Blaylock

6. Your Legacy: What Will You Leave for Others? — 67
Patricia Cheeseboro

7. Mirror, Mirror: Look Inside — 79
Tamera Swan Mason

8. Avoiding Toxic Relationships — 89
L. Denise Jackson

TABLE OF CONTENTS
–CONTINUED–

9. The Chameleon: The Art of Transition and Change — 101
   Rosemary Medel

10. Victim vs. Survivor — 113
    Violet Mathis

11. 15 Strategies for Overcoming Negative Thinking — 125
    Karen Brundage-Johnson

12. Creating Your Space for Peace — 137
    Linda Farr

13. Building Self-Esteem — 151
    Dr. Mary Ann Alexander-Wilford

14. Marching to the Beat of Your Own Drum — 161
    Dr. Daphne Young

15. Pretty Is As Pretty Does: Living a Life of Purpose — 171
    Michele' Lawlis

16. The Portrayal of Women in the Media — 187
    Sharyn Lynn Yonkman

17. When You've Fallen or Failed — 199
    Sherron Sparks Hain

TABLE OF CONTENTS
–CONTINUED–

18. Healthy Eating: Getting Fit — 215
    Heidi Santiago

19. Where Do You Go From Here? Choosing Your Future — 225
    Ruby Ashley

20. Self-Talk: Becoming Your Own Best Friend — 237
    Martha Kirby

21. Your Mirror Reflection: What Are You Attracting? — 245
    Jane Denner

22. Women vs. Women: How to Overcome Gossip & Sabotage — 261
    Mardi Allen

23. Getting Well: Handling Our Emotions — 273
    Hannah Crutcher

24. Living Your Dreams — 285
    Brenda J. McDowell-Holmes

25. Dealing with Sadness and Grief — 297
    Dorothy E. Everhart

ABOUT THE AUTHOR

Linda Eastman

Linda Ellis Eastman is President and CEO of The Professional Woman Network (PWN), an International Training and Consulting Organization on Women's Issues. She has designed seminars which have been presented in China, the former Soviet Union, South Africa, the Phillipines, and attended by individuals in the United States from such firms as McDonalds, USA Today, Siemens-Westinghouse, the Pentagon, the Department of Defense, and the United States Department of Education.

An expert on women's issues, Ms. Eastman has certified and trained over one thousand women to start consulting/seminar businesses originating from such countries as Pakistan, the Ukraine, Antigua, Canada, Mexico, Zimbabwe, Nigeria, Bermuda, Jamaica, Costa Rica, England, South Africa, Malaysia, and Kenya. Founded in 1982 by Linda Ellis Eastman, The Professional Woman Network is committed to educating women on a global basis regarding, self-esteem, confidence building, stress management, and emotional, mental, spiritual and physical wellness.

Ms. Eastman has been featured in USA Today and listed in Who's Who of American Women, as well as Who's Who of International Leaders. In addition to women's issues, Ms. Eastman speaks internationally regarding the importance of human respect as it relates to race, color, culture, age, and gender. She will be facilitating an international conference where speakers and participants from many nations will be able to discuss issues that are unique to women on a global basis.

Linda Ellis Eastman is also founder of The Professional Woman Speakers Bureau and The Professional Woman Coaching Institute. Ms. Eastman has dedicated her businesses to increasing the self-esteem and personal dignity of women and youth around the world.

Contact
The Professional Woman Network
P.O. Box 333
Prospect, KY 40059
(502) 566-9900
lindaeastman@prodigy.net
www.prowoman.net
www.protrain.net

INTRODUCTION

Linda Ellis Eastman

As women, we tend to place important emphasis upon our outward appearances. We follow the newest fashion trends and make certain that we are polished in our image. However, what about the inner self?

This book has been written to provide guidance and support for women who seek to have a more holistic view of themselves, embracing not only their outer selves, but taking a journey deep within to the core of their very being.

Women are emotional beings. Emotions should be embraced as a gift as these emotions provide women with empathy for others and a deep-sensing of what others feel. However, these same emotions may take women on a roller coaster ride.

This book is designed to bring the reader emotional balance while providing guidelines about the important journey to self-discovery, increased self-esteem, and building a healthy relationship with others and YOURSELF.

Twenty five gifted consultants, trainers, and coaches have written a powerful book for you, the reader. May each chapter bring you closer to accepting yourself and provide the roadmap for life's often challenging emotional journey.

BEYOND THE BODY! DEVELOPING INNER BEAUTY

ABOUT THE AUTHOR

TAMMY McDONALD

Dr. Tammy Y. McDonald is President and CEO of Youth & Family Alliance, Inc, a Community Support Agency assisting mental health and substance abuse consumers. Tammy is also a certified life coach, behavioral modification specialist, and motivational speaker of women's issues. Tammy holds a Bachelor's Degree in International Studies, a Master's Degree in Counseling Studies, and a PhD. in Behavioral Science. Tammy's career path has been nourished by a variety of creative detours. Tammy originally wanted to be an Arabic translator, but after working with behaviorally challenged adolescents and young adults she began a career in the Human Services arena, specifically serving consumers with mental health diagnoses.

Tammy is a fabulous short-story writer and is in the process of cultivating two short-stories for publication. She is also a great story teller, and her stories touch people's hearts in various ways. Her writings have been known to facilitate an experience, initiate sincere notions leading to insights, new perspectives and at times significant breakthroughs. "My grandmother, who I call Granny, unknowingly had to be the biggest influence on me creatively. Through her life stories, she taught me the importance of comprehending and grasping information in an effort to recall an experience to aid not only myself but others as well. I kept a diary as a child, and was always writing stories and poems." In 1997, Tammy began immersing herself in learning about the lives of ordinary and extraordinary women. Tammy was empowered by growing up as a female in this country, and continues to communicate and uplift women from different racial, geographic, and socioeconomic backgrounds. Tammy is happily married and with three beautiful children.

Contact:
Dr. Tammy McDonald
PO Box 509
Castle Hayne, NC 28429
Email: mcdon910@aol.com

ONE

MENTAL CLUTTER

By Dr. Tammy McDonald

Initially, when I selected this topic, I thought to myself, "Mental clutter, this will be easy." I will simply teach people how to reorganize and declutter their lives by training them to utilize daily agendas and create the almighty 'to-do list,' thus creating an environment that would automatically eliminate their mental clutter. Well, I was then posed with a question from one of my client's. "With all that you do, how is it that you are able to remain so happy and stable all the time?" After I answered that question, I realized that I had purposely made choices in my life so I could live a life without mental clutter and unwanted drama.

In order to understand clutter, one must truly grasp the concept of how clutter is truly defined. The Webster's dictionary defines clutter as an untidy collection of objects, or a condition of disorderliness or overcrowding. Armed with this vital piece of information, we will begin to explore how clutter can impact our overall progression or regression in our lives. Although this definition is accurate, I personally define mental clutter as the emotional unrest and disorder, ultimately creating baggage that weaves itself into the foundational structure of our mental state, thus creating pillars of weakness that affects the overall mental state of existence. The one amazing phenomenon that I have come to realize is that on some level, everyone will always be exposed to mental clutter; its how you choose to handle this monster that will determine how badly you want to exist without mental shackles.

In order to explain this process, I made the comparison to deep cleaning and restoring a home. If done correctly, each step of the cleaning process could elevate us to the mental clarity that we are seeking to live a clutter-free life.

Identifying the Clutter

Life has taught us that we can't fix what we can't see. Well, in order to start to free ourselves of mental clutter, we have to identify or acknowledge the clutter. Of all of the processes that you will address, this by far may be the hardest. This process forces you to come face-to-face with all of the emotional monsters that may have had you mentally running like a fugitive in your mind for years, or even decades. Although they are endless, I will touch on a few that may have played a leading role in controlling your mental thoughts at some point in your life.

Fears

The first clutter factor is fear. In my opinion, this small four-letter word is packed with power, because it can immediately stop any kind of progress. Oftentimes, we refuse to grow and develop because of fear that we will receive criticism, or we may not seek the desired approval that we think we need from others. I have found that in many cases, fear has been powerful enough to limit and paralyze individuals, because they were unable to see beyond the scope of what society perceives as normal (thinking big, or living out a dream). As a result of living our lives in fear, we choose to clutter our minds with excuses as to why we should continue to live substandard, pitiful lives instead of catapulting ourselves to greatness.

Failure

Society unfortunately has quietly imprinted in our minds that to fail at something that we have tried implies that we have lost, or that we are unable to perform at an acceptable rate. As a result of this judgment, we tend to operate in what I refer to as the "caution lane." This particular clutter factor has a direct impact on the way we view challenges and opportunities, because failure is an instant success blocker, and its intimidation keeps us stagnated and feeling that there is no need to try because success is not within reach.

Grudges

Having a list of people who have hurt you and who you refuse to forgive translates into mental clutter. Grudges have the potential to cripple individuals because it acts as an anchor that we carry around. Oftentimes, individuals feel that they have forgiven others that have hurt or betrayed them, only to have swept unresolved issues under a rug in hopes that they never have to see or deal with them again. However, this unsuccessful concept only works until you trip over the lump under the rug. It's important that we keep in mind that, as long as there are people walking this Earth with you, you will be hurt, however, refusing to let their words or actions invade and infest your emotional well-being will allow you to remain focused on your personnel growth and independence.

Just Settling

This particular clutter factor is extremely important to me because, at some point in our lives, we will find ourselves at this juncture. Settling occurs when we have found comfort in our lives, or convinced ourselves that we aren't doing "so bad" which translates to, we are not willing to try and grow, or we are afraid to move to the next phase in our lives. As we journey through life, we must remember that there is a season for everything. There is a season for planting and prepping (our dreams), and there is a season that we must nurture and tend to our harvest as it grows. Eventually, there will also be a season for our harvest. It is vitally important that we are aware of this time, because if you are not, you will have wasted valuable time, energy, and effort on a field of dreams and aspirations that will surely die because you opted to settle and refused to enjoy the fruits of your labor.

Regrets

I find it sad when I listen to individuals point out the list of accomplishments that they wanted to achieve but didn't because of events and circumstances that occurred in their lives. Whether it was the need to take care of someone, or that famous line, "I put my life on hold for the sake of the family," regrets are mental clutters that help promote "the poor me syndrome." When individuals are unable to achieve their goals or aspirations for the sake of… , then it provides an immediate and unconscious excuse for not stepping out to at least try, or it could be another way of quietly saying that you are scared.

Negative Self-Talk

At some point in our lives, we have all been guilty of this clutter factor. Negative self-talk tends to roll off our tongues as easily as it is to place an order at our favorite restaurant. It has been my experience that negatively putting yourself down, or calling yourself names, is extremely damaging to your self-image, because we have the potential to expose ourselves to negative self-talk more frequently. Sadly enough, most of this negativity is done unknowingly or unconsciously. It is vital that we understand that, when we expose ourselves to this form of self-inflicted abuse, we are disregarding our own self-worth and value.

Negative Talk from Others

It is my strong belief that negative talk from others cuts to the core and shreds our self-esteem. When we allow people to "abuse" us verbally, then we unknowingly become scarred. Whether it's an individual close to you, or a casual person jokingly interacting with you, never allow or accept them putting you down or calling you out of your name; when you do, you are co-signing these thoughts and perceptions, thus increasing the potential for you to internalize and adopt these as your thoughts.

Now that we have come face-to-face with the stains on the floors and walls, the overflowing trash, the unwanted dust bunnies, hidden dirt in the corners, and the overcrowded closets, take a moment to gather yourself. It's really easy to become overwhelmed and shut down when you are evaluating the big picture, but don't worry, we will get through this together. The first thing that you must do is take a true inventory of your life and ask yourself, "Is my current situation something that looks and feels right to me, or can I use a change?" If you want more for your life, then the answer is easy. But, I want to caution you that the changes that you are choosing to undertake won't happen overnight. Remaining consistent will be the key to success as you work to declutter and reorganize your life. Now, let's pull up our sleeves and let's get to work!

Manifestations

As we deal with mental clutter, there are many ways that we will, and do manifest these mental clutter factors. For some individuals, anger exists because of the underlying fear that they have failed to explore or acknowledge, thus leaving them with many unresolved issues. While others find themselves consumed with anger and frustration, particularly when they reflect back on their lives and conclude that they have failed more times than they have succeeded. Regrets have the potential to take over individuals who are overwhelmed with their life's direction. Negativity is another manifestation that has the power to impact not only you, but also individuals around you, because it causes you to lash out and inflict self-harm to yourself. It is, in my opinion, that when one allows negativity to enter into their lives, then there is the potential to become self-destructive, because hopelessness is the driving emotion. Bitterness is another manifestation that takes the forefront when we are not willing to let grudges go. This manifestation is an example of how we allow individuals who have caused hurt and created devastation in our lives to gain power over our thoughts and emotions, even after they have gone. It is my belief that we are unable to detach from these emotions or feelings because we feel that it is our duty or responsibility to hold on to the negative energy as a means of attempting to hurt the individual, only to harm ourselves in the end.

Now that we have identified all of our mental clutter, and have taken into account how it has altered and changed our lives, the only step left to do is to find the clarity that you desire by "CLEANING UP!" This process can be somewhat of a challenge, because you are deciding to change the behaviors that have gotten you to this point. Part of this challenge will be the new direction in which your new life changes must transpire. Previously, the transformations were occurring within, which offered some sense of privacy. Now, these inner changes must be reflected outwardly, allowing the transformation to become visible to those around you. You may not think that this will pose a problem, but the one truth that I know is the one thing harder than change, is wondering or worrying about how others will accept your change. During this rebirthing process, you will find out who your true supporters are, and who wants you stuck in a miserable state of clutter. The key to success as you begin this process is remaining strong, committed, and grounded! Initially, you will find that some of your days will be easy, and some days you are going to want to simply give up. But, remember to continue to tell yourself that you are worth this makeover, and at the end of the day you are getting closer to living a life filled with purpose and happiness.

Tools Needed to Declutter

Dust is the small blanket of particles that settle on objects. For the dust that we see, we will occasionally wipe it away so that the surface is presentable; while often times, unseen dust will go unaddressed until we are forced to deal with it, when we are arranging. I equate this to living a life filled with lies and deceit. Often times we want to present to the outside world that everything is "wonderful," and we will do anything to preserve this image. When it comes to dusting, I've found that a feather duster has the ability to remove the dust, but from one particular area to another, or releasing the dust into the air. I often relate this to life when we have to deal with or confront stressors in our lives. Instead of dealing with the issues, we tend to spread them around by putting them off, in hopes that they will fix themselves. Interesting enough, the best technique for picking up dust is to spray a furniture polish on the surface, and then wipe away the dust with a cloth. During this process, it is evident that the dust has been captured, because the dust sticks to the rag and is successfully picked up. In relation to life, it is vital that you are approaching stressors that occur with the intention of facing, addressing and resolving the issue. By doing so, you gain the confidence that you need to take on all stressors that want to settle in your life.

While on the subject of polishing, I would like to address the importance of regular polishing. You need to make sure that the furniture around you is continuously dust free so that the beauty can shine through, making us proud for others to see, despite their opinions. Applying this to your life is no different; so often the negativity that we experience starts to affect our natural shine and glow. Making sure that you are showing yourself the utmost respect is essential. This tolerance also extends to others, as well. Sadly enough, we spend our lives making sure that we are closely monitoring what we are putting into our bodies by refraining from smoking, or sitting in the non-smoking section of a restaurant, not drinking or using drugs, and eating healthy foods. However, we are extremely neglectful and careless when it comes to allowing the negative junk from ourselves and others to enter into our minds, and manifest into extreme negativity. Your mind is a part of your body! Make it your duty to take care of it just as you take care of all your other parts. When you neglect your mind, your body will eventually pay the price.

Three tools that will be helpful as you work to declutter your life are the broom, mop, and vacuum. These tools are wonderful because they gather, clean, and suck up dirt, producing instant cleaning gratification. How does this apply to life you ask? Well, by deciding that you want to live a powerful life with freedom, one must take these tools out of the corner, and actually put them to use. To start, one must acknowledge that no one is perfect, and that mistakes are just another way of getting one step closer to success. So, as you sweep the mental floors of your mind, take inventory of all of your failures, and don't be afraid to try it again. Only this time, think outside of the box to achieve greatness. Once the sweeping is completed, we need to give our floors a major cleaning. By taking the mop and scrubbing away all of the marks and stains, your floors will reveal a clean sanitary environment that aids in keeping the environment safe. In our lives, this can be equated to when we are working to rid ourselves of regrets; from this point on, make a commitment to achieve all of your goals. For many of us, pursuing our aspirations may need to take on a unique or individualized path because of circumstances currently in our lives, but these should never be reasons for not maximizing your desire to live out your dreams. Now that your mental floors have been cleaned, make sure that the steps that you take are ones without regret; no matter what you do, don't forget you are destined for greatness. However, it's up to you to determine how badly you want it.

Now that we have cleaned our floors, we must turn our attention to the carpets. The last tool that we will need to declutter mental clutter is the vacuum. When vacuuming occurs, seen and unseen dirt is captured and trapped into a bag or cylinder, thus leaving a clean and inviting surface for all to enjoy. I have found that we use the vacuum when we are looking for an instant means to remove dirt from the floor. I have related this to living in fear when it comes to eliminating the mental clutter in our lives. Instead of running or avoiding the obstacles that we are afraid of, try coming face-to-face with the intentions and dealing with them until you have overcome the fear or eliminated it in its entirety. I have also found that if you tell yourself that, "fear is not an option," and that "problems are only situations needing solutions," then operate under the "fake it, until you make it" mentality. Then there is nothing that will stop you, but you! Never forget, you don't have to be a victim of your circumstances unless you allow yourself to be.

Now, the last tool has to be one of the most important ones, because it is what I like to call the "closure tool." The trash can is the collector or holder of all the trash that you have collected. I am particularly excited when I apply this tool to life. Before we go any further, I think that you should stop and pat yourself on the back, because you have made a conscious decision to let go of all of the clutter keeping you from moving to the next level. So far we have been able to capture a lot of clutter by dusting, polishing, sweeping, mopping, and vacuuming. Now, before we take a break, we have one more task to complete. Take one last look around at the piles of clutter that may have collected in the corners or closets; the specific clutter that I am referring to are the grudges that you have refused to let go of. Despite all of the hard work that you have done, if you are not willing to let go of all of the hurt, hatred, and vengeful feelings that have overcome you at some point in your life, all of your work will have been in vain. This mental clutter can be hard for some people, because grudges can surface at any time without warning, and take over your thinking process on every level. In order to overcome these feelings, you must firmly tell yourself that you hate that you were hurt, but it can't be undone. However, in order to move to the next level, you must place all of the hurt in the trash can, and be willing to leave it there. When you refuse to let go of the mental invasions, specifically the feelings or people responsible for those feelings of hurt, then you become a prisoner, which will hinder how you move into the next transitional phase of your life.

Mental Makeover

As I stated previously, the first step to declutter is deciding that you want to be free of the mental poison and toxicants that you are taking into your body on a daily basis. I like to refer to this stage as the "sorting process" or the "mental makeover." Although there are many steps to creating the perfect makeover, I will discuss five steps that you may find helpful in this transformation to greatness. The first step is to get excited about your life, and everything that you aspire to become. If you are one of those individuals who have identified your goals in life, then make sure that you are working everyday to achieve or perfect your skills. For the individuals who are still working to find your way, don't stress, simply ask yourself, what it is that you want to do when you grow up, and promise yourself that you are going to work to achieve your dreams (put it in writing if you need to). The key to overcoming any mental clutter and remaining clutter-free is remaining excited about your life. You are your greatest cheerleader, so make sure that you are cheering yourself on every step of the way. Even when your days are trying, never stop cheering! The next step to a successful makeover is remembering that atmosphere is everything. Atmosphere is everything. In order to create a calm, serene environment, you must work to reinvent yourself. Keep in mind that you will have to arrange and rearrange many of your thoughts and behaviors until the flow or layout is pleasing to you. In order to achieve this goal, you may need to seek the assistance of a Professional Life Coach or a Behavior Specialist. This support will be helpful during this particular process because of the presenting stress factors you will be forced to deal with as you work to eliminate habits, and even old friends or associates that have been in your life in order to make room for growth and development. Often times, changing and reorganizing can be intimidating for many of us because of the ambiguity that exists regarding change. Despite these fears, one should never be afraid to try something new. Now, the unique aspect about trying something different is that, if it does not work for you, you can always make a change. Once you have identified the look that works for you, remember that less is always more. What I am referring to is the need to make sure that you are being very careful about the individuals that you allow in your precious space on a regular basis. Remember, negative people produce negative garbage, hurtful people produce painful toxins; make sure that you keep in mind that eliminating negativity in your life will help you remain positive and full of clarity. During this process, we find ourselves with bags of garbage. In order to gain the ultimate experience for your mental makeover, you must be willing to do the hardest aspect of this entire makeover—take the trash to the curb and walk away. By doing this, you are able to take off the mental weights that have held you in place for so long. The final stage of the mental makeover is to simply enjoy all of your hard work. Most importantly, make sure that you take time daily to acknowledge all of your hard work and dedication, and strive to go beyond societal scopes to live a life of happiness that you created because you were determined that you were worth it.

Mental Maintenance

Making the decision to go through one's mental home and expose all of the unresolved issues, hidden baggage, and layers of emotions can be a challenge for anyone, and should not be taken lightly. Despite the many unpleasant waves of emotions that you will experience as you journey through this process, I promise that the results will be worth it! The final stage of the emotional makeover is mental maintenance. Once you have journeyed to the place where you are truly happy and satisfied with who you are and all that you have and are working to accomplish, then it is important that you remain there. In order to do this, maintaining clarity on a daily basis will be essential. Immediately address anything that clutters your mental state. Don't allow anyone or anything to make you regress or overturn all of your hard work. Talk to yourself; when you find yourself getting negative, immediately stop yourself, and replace your negative self-talk with positive self-talk. For those of you who are thinking that you are too old to change, don't worry, it's a behavior, and it can be changed. The final thing that you should do is to listen to yourself; the mind, body and spirit must always be aligned. Whether it's praying, doing deep breathing techniques, exercising, relaxing, or simply taking a private moment with yourself to find clarity in this very demanding and fast paced world, always remember, we only get one chance on this Earth, and I think that it is essential that we show God how much we love him by loving ourselves the way he has always and will always love us.

ABOUT THE AUTHOR

ALICE J. MAXIN

Alice J. Maxin is President and Founder of **Panorama Coaching**, a company dedicated to helping clients achieve success through vision and planning. She is a professional life coach, certified by the Professional Woman Network (PWN), an international consulting and training organization.

With a Master's degree in education from Clarion University of PA, Alice taught in public schools for over twenty-five years before changing careers in 1995. She became a labor relations specialist for Pennsylvania State Education Association (PSEA/NEA), negotiating and advocating for school employees across southwestern PA. Proficient in assertive behavior and communication skills, Alice exhibits expertise in facilitation, training, coaching, problem solving and trust within the workplace environment. This led to the origination of **Panorama Coaching**. Alice is a certified trainer for Basic Leadership Skills, Women's Leadership, Assertiveness, Women's Issues, Emotional Wellness, Organizational Skills (including time management), and Training the Trainer. Her customize-designed programs for both businesses and individuals provide the foundation for **Panorama Coaching**.

In addition to being a member of the PWN International Advisory Board, Alice belongs to the PWN Speakers Bureau and the National Association for Female Executives. She received recognition for her professional successes in Who's Who Among American Teachers, Who's Who in American Education, and Who's Who of American Women. Alice co-authored two PWN books: *Woman's Journey to Wellness: Mind, Body, and Spirit* and *Beyond the Body: Developing Inner Beauty*. She is also co-author of the final book in the PWN collection: *The Baby Boomer's Handbook*.

Alice enjoys spending time with her granddaughter Erin and volunteering for the Armstrong County Community Foundation's early literacy initiative. She also organized the first support group for the Restless Legs Syndrome Foundation in western PA, Pittsburgh North.

Her company, **Panorama Coaching**, achieves widespread respect for its useful applications in the professional environment and for continued relevance in its clients' lives. Whether you are an individual seeking guidance from a personal coach or a business, hospital, or school searching for just the right program, let your horizons expand and the view will become clearer by contacting **Panorama Coaching** for all of your training and coaching needs.

Contact:
Panorama Coaching
Alice J. Maxin
143 Sportsman Road
Leechburg, PA 15656
(724) 295-4121
 E-Mail: alice@panoramacoach.com
Website: www.panoramacoach.com

TWO

A BILL OF RIGHTS FOR THE ASSERTIVE WOMAN

By Alice Maxin

"Never grow a wishbone, daughter, where your backbone ought to be."
— Clementine Paddleford (columnist)

Imagine being a woman in 1787. The Constitution of the United States was adopted by the Constitutional Convention and signed by George Washington and more than twenty other men. Times were difficult: cold, dreary winters with food provisions only from what the family preserved, livestock that survived, and game provided by the men of the village. You, as a woman, struggled to keep the home fires burning, the children clothed, clean and fed, and your husband comfortable after his long day of hunting. Also, imagine having no voice in how the government affected you, because you did not have the right to vote in elections until the Nineteenth Amendment to that Constitution passed in August of 1920.

Fast-forward to today and examine the Constitution again. There is a Bill of Rights attached to the document. Yet, specific rights for an assertive woman appear nowhere in the legal annals. Therefore, three questions come to mind:

1. Where <u>is</u> an assertive woman's Bill of Rights written?

2. Who must abide by these rights?

3. What rights <u>do</u> you have as an assertive woman?

First, you need to identify the term "assertive." Listing synonyms for the word is a good place to start. Record below at least three words you associate with the term "assertive":

1. _____

2. _____

3. _____

Did any of these words appear on your list?
- Self-confident
- Self-assured
- Confident

- Firm
- Forceful
- Strong
- Courageous

All represent facets of an assertive personality. You can probably name many more. Keep them in mind as you explore your rights in this chapter.

1. Where is an assertive woman's Bill of Rights written?

    In short, nowhere. It is philosophical in nature and can be attributed to men as well.

2. Who must abide by them?

    Again, it is a short answer: Another assertive person hopefully will recognize the importance of your rights and reciprocate the courtesy. In an ideal world, everyone would honor each other's rights.

3. What rights do you have as an assertive woman?

    This is the substance of the rest of the chapter. Describe what you feel are your rights insofar as being assertive. _____

In providing leadership training to hundreds of women over the last twenty years, I emphasized that one of the cornerstones of leadership was the recognition of your rights as an assertive person. We discussed the differences between assertive and aggressive, and the characteristics of a passive person. We looked at the following rights and many lively discussions followed. Please feel free to add your own comments to each of these rights.

1. You have the right to do anything, as long as it does not infringe upon someone else's rights.

   In other words, you must not break the Ten Commandments or the laws of man. Can you think of a time when someone violated your rights? What happened? How did you feel? How did you react? Write about that time and your feelings regarding it. _____
   _____
   _____

   Now imagine yourself politely, yet confidently, addressing that person and asking for an explanation. Will you grant forgiveness, if it is requested? Why, or why not? _____
   _____

   A self-assured woman will find a way to move forward, learn from the experience, and set a good example for others to follow.

2. You have the right to your own opinion, and to express it without intentionally hurting others.

   To always say what others expect you to say is not being true to yourself. An assertive woman will weigh and measure the facts of a situation, and develop her own opinion. Without inflicting purposeful hurt on another person, she will express her thoughts in a timely, confident manner. Timeliness is key, if her opinion is to have merit.

People form perceptions based on their attitude toward your behavior. Although you cannot control their perception and attitude, you **are** in charge of your own words and behavior. If someone perceives your opinion as being rude or hurtful, you, as an assertive woman, will do your best to repair the situation by changing how you express yourself. You need not relinquish your position, only your delivery.

3. You have the right to say NO.

"No" is a complete answer to someone's request. If you are asked "why not", then also stating your reason is appropriate. For example - a friend calls and wants you to go to the movies with her that night. You promised yourself an evening of uninterrupted time with your spouse. You have the right to say, "No, I cannot join you," without having to explain why. If the friend persists, you might expand your response to include, "I have another commitment." A detailed outline of your evening and a promise never to turn the friend down again is succumbing to the pressure to be passive.

Write about a time when you said "No". What happened as a result? Did you stand your ground?_____

4. You have the right to say, "I do not know."

Have you ever asked someone a question and realized that she did not know the answer? Her response was nothing more than a verbal essay in run-around talk. Why do you think people do this? Write your thoughts here. _____
_____

An assertive person has the confidence <u>not</u> to be all-knowing. Most people will respect an "I do not know" response IF it is followed by "I will find out (or decide) and get back to you by_____ (within a reasonable time period)." It is imperative that you keep your word and give the information requested by the stated time.

5. You have the right to say, "I do not understand."

Whether you are negotiating a contract, getting directions from a gas station attendant, or accepting an assignment from your boss, it is vital that both parties comprehend what is being considered. An assertive woman clarifies what she hears before taking action.

Saying you do not understand does not mean that you are not intelligent. It does not mean that you are uncaring. It does mean that you care enough to respond correctly. Confidence grows when you seek clarification and knowledge.

There are numerous ways to check for accuracy in understanding. Circle which response an assertive woman would make in the following.

I. A salesperson offers you a ten percent rebate if and when you have made a deal.

   a. "Okay." You walk away, mentally wondering what constitutes a deal.

   b. "I will agree to that amount of rebate once I understand what the terms of the deal will be. Please explain what you mean."

   c. "That's not good enough for me." You hope she offers more.

II. The gas station attendant, in response to your inquiry, says, "Turn left at the stop sign in town and just keep driving till you see lots of cows near Joe Green's farmhouse."

   a. You say "thanks" and drive off wondering how many stop signs are in the town, and if he meant the first one, or not.

   b. "How many cows will I see?"

   c. "Is it the first stop sign? How far do I need to drive before I see the cows in Joe Green's pasture? Is the farmhouse on the left or right side of the road?"

III. The boss assigns you another report to do and wants it done differently than all the others you have done before.

   a. "I am not sure I understand what you mean by 'differently'. Please explain what your expectations are so that I can do my job properly."

   b. "Okay." You wonder if the boss even knows how the other reports were done, and why this one has to be different. You pray that you get it right.

   c. "I'll give it a shot and hope it suits you."

The assertive responses are I-b, II-c, and III-a. How did you do? If your answers were different, ask yourself why.

6. You have the right to judge your own behavior and to take responsibility for it.

You are in charge of your life and the decisions you make about it. If you believe in what you are doing, you need not apologize for standing up for those beliefs.

Judgments about your behavior come through trial and error. They should not be a system of right and wrong, should and should not, would have, could have, etc. Taking responsibility for their actions is what adults do to be dependable. A solid foundation in the belief of a Higher Power will aid you in this task.

7. You have the right to prioritize your own life.

Have you ever asked yourself, "When is it time for me?" What was your response to that question?_____
_____

If it seems as though your plans always take second, third or twentieth place to everyone else's, it is time to ask why.

Is everyone else more important than you are? Of course not. However, if you always relinquish what you want, then you are sending the message to those around you that your plans, your time, and your health are not important.

There will be times of crisis when all else must take a back seat to whatever is driving the situation. For example, your spouse is rushed to the hospital with a possible heart attack. Although you promised yourself a night out with the girls in just two hours, your plans must be postponed.

On the other hand, some people thrive on crisis, and view most events in their lives as predicaments of colossal proportions. You do not have to succumb to the pressure of their urgency.

An assertive woman knows that her physical, mental, and emotional well-being depend on her choices. The choice to make your own decisions about what is important, urgent, and necessary in your life is the framework for letting others know they cannot rule you. You also send the message that you value yourself. If you do not hold yourself in high esteem, how can you expect others to view you with appreciation?

What events are on the horizon of your life in the next day or two? Next week? Next month? List them now:

_____

_____

_____

Go back and prioritize them as to their importance and urgency. Ask yourself who decides what is pressing and important. The answer for an assertive woman is, "I am the one who decides."

8. You have the right to change your mind.

To change your mind – is that not a woman's prerogative?

You have the right to change your mind about a decision you make. More facts become available. Circumstances change. Opinion and attitude affect your choices.

For example, you volunteer at a staff meeting to single-handedly take on three new accounts. Now you find that your other work is falling behind and your family life is nonexistent because of the time-consuming tasks these new accounts require. Do you have a choice? Yes, you do! What would be your course of action? Choose one of the options below.

A. You continue to do all the work alone. As usual, you just swallow hard, cry in private, ignore your family, and generally complain to anyone who will listen about how unfair life is.

B. You approach your boss and seek advice as to what company priority you are to place on each account. You also ask for assistance if the situation warrants.

C. You quit your job.

If you chose B, you understand the necessity and correctness of changing your initial response. An assertive woman is also confident enough to know when she needs help – and to ask for it.

On the other hand, changing your mind after <u>every</u> decision you make could be construed as passive or passive-aggressive behavior. You, as an assertive woman, weigh your options and choose your course of action accordingly, changing your mind, if necessary, to maintain your rights and dignity.

9. You have the right to make mistakes.

Mistakes are inaccuracies, slip-ups, boo-boos and blunders. They are not wrongdoings. They are only errors in judgment and decision. It is the assignment of the arbitrary terms "right" and "wrong" that people attach to your actions and words that make you feel self-conscious. If you are the one who beats yourself up after each decision you make, STOP. Think of what you are doing to your self-esteem.

The only regret attached to mistakes is the one you will have if you do not learn from the mistake. Let your mistakes become knowledge stepping-stones. The future will repeat the past if you do not grow with experience.

A case in point is the den mother whose turn it was to supply homemade cookies for her son's Cub Scout meeting that night. She mistakenly thought her donation was due the next week. When they arrived at the meeting and twenty sets of hungry eyes saw her empty hands, she realized her slip-up. She apologized to the troop, excused herself after the other parents began the meeting, drove to a nearby convenience store, and returned with Oreos in time for the snack break. All were happy.

A passive person would have profusely apologized at least ten times, made many excuses for her mistake, and promised to bring homemade donuts for the rest of the year! An aggressive person would have laughed and told the children they were out of shape anyway, and did not need any cookies. The assertive mother took responsibility for her mistake and learned from the experience: she now writes her scheduled treat days on the calendar, and then checks the calendar well ahead of time.

10. You have the right to make requests of others, as long as you remember that they also have the right to say NO.

As a self-assured woman, you recognize when you need assistance with a task or an obligation. You have the right to ask others for assistance, not to fulfill your commitment, but to aid in your quest for completion. For the same reasons whereby you have the right to say NO, others also can invoke the same privilege.

You, the confident woman, will respect their rights and not try to bully a more positive response from them. You remember their right to privacy and their need to take care of themselves. You honor their dignity and, in return, place yourself in a position of respect.

11. You have the right to be non-assertive if a situation so warrants.

You might ask yourself, "Why would I want to be non-assertive if my goal is to live my life with confidence?"

Two situations come to mind in which an assertive response would not be the most effective one.

A. One night you are walking alone to your car after working late. A stranger approaches you with a demand for money. The interloper has a gun or a knife and threatens to use it if you do not hand over your purse or wallet. It would be disastrous, even fatal, if you assertively answered, "I respectfully do not agree with your demand. Let's talk it over and see if we might develop a plan that satisfies both of us." It is time for passivity. Even though you do not want to lose your money and credit cards, you must hand them over to have any chance of ending the situation without further provocation. You can replace the cash and cards; you cannot replace your life. A broken ego is better than a broken body!

B. At work, you are carrying supplies down the hall past a management business meeting in the conference room. You smell smoke and then see it coming from the copy room two doors away. To knock politely on the door, excuse yourself for interrupting, and ask if you might have a minute to address the group, would be to put lives needlessly in danger.

Now is the time for aggression. Pound on the door. Yell "Fire". Insist that everyone leave right now. The situation necessitates aggressive words and action. A confident woman chooses when she is assertive, and decides when circumstances call for passive or aggressive action. Recognizing when different responses are appropriate comes with practice and maturity.

12. You have the right to maintain your dignity, as long as your motive is open and honest.

Maintaining your dignity ensures an assertive reaction to life. If you do not respect yourself, how can you expect others to value you? Sincere, straightforward intentions cause families, friends, colleagues, and even casual acquaintances, to view you as trustworthy. Hidden agendas have no place in an assertive woman's life. Dignity means self-respect, poise, self-esteem, decorum. Preserving it by being honest will give you the courage to lead an assertive life.

These twelve assertive rights represent a framework for establishing yourself as a viable, worthy human being. They are, by nature, for all people to experience. Inner beauty radiates from those who live assertively, and respect the rights of others.

Recommended Readings and Resources

Assertiveness: Getting What You Want Without Being Pushy by National Press Publications

The Communication Coach edited by Jeffrey Tobe

Nice Girls Don't Get the Corner Office by Lois P. Frankel, Ph.D.

Talking From 9 to 5 by Deborah Tannen, Ph.D.

Tender Power by Sherry Suib Cohen

Women and the Art of Negotiating by Juliet Nierenberg and Irene S. Ross

We the People: The Citizen and the Constitution by Center for Civic Education

ABOUT THE AUTHOR

APRIL B. JONES

April Jones is President and CEO of A Plan For You, LLC. She conducts workshops and seminars that have been presented throughout the United States and abroad. The workshops and seminars conducted by the institute consist of topics such as: Women in Management, Women as Leaders, The Superwoman Syndrome, Leadership Skills, The Assertive Woman, Customer Service, Diversity and Emotional Wellness for Women. Ms. Jones has been certified by The Professional Woman Network as a Professional Coach and Diversity Consultant.

Ms. Jones' knowledge of business and professionalism is supported by working with corporations, non-profit and charity organizations. She has over 14 years of experience with the U.S. Federal Government in information technology and management, 7+ years consulting experience with churches and small business firms.

Among her many accomplishments, Ms. Jones has co-authored two books, been recognized by Strathmore's Who's Who Global Network for Outstanding Professionals, holds a Masters Degrees in Telecommunication and Information Systems from Capitol College in Laurel, Maryland and a Masters Degree in Information Management with a specialization in Government from Syracuse University in Syracuse, New York.

Contact:
A Plan for You, LLC.
1282 Smallwood Drive W. #332
Waldorf, MD 20603
(301) 710.5421
Email: info@aplanforyou.org
www.aplanforyou.org
www.isthatyourhouse.com
www.protrain.net

THREE

SETTING PERSONAL GOALS

By April B. Jones

Have you ever overheard someone sharing their desire to start a business, but when asked what type of business or service they will be providing, the answer is, "I don't know." Or, "I'm not sure yet." Better than that, have you ever said to someone (or to yourself), "I want to go back to school to complete my degree by the time I turn _____ " (whatever the age is). "I want to make more money." "If only I had the office with four windows." "If I could just lose 50 pounds." Sweeping generalizations like these often lead to personal disappointment and frustration. Our thoughts are all over the place, with no aim, direction or actual target. Whether good or bad, right or wrong, most of us are goal chasers of undeveloped goals and desires. Goal chasing comes from misunderstanding what you want for your life, or what path to take in life.

Webster's dictionary defines a goal as the purpose toward which an endeavor is directed. Does this definition match the generalizations listed above? How can you take a basic idea and turn it into a personal goal? What benefit will setting personal goals provide?

It is my desire that, by the end of this chapter, you will be armed with useful guidelines that will allow you to establish and maintain a healthy strategy for developing and achieving personal goals. You will have an outline to develop the blueprint for your life.

Why Set Personal Goals?

It is crucial to your inner development, growth and esteem that you not allow yourself to be subject to activities that steal your time, drain your energy, deplete your bank account, devalue your self-respect, or diminish your self-esteem. Are you in control of your life's destiny? Do you have a clear understanding of what you want to achieve in the future? Do you have a detailed plan of action to achieve those things? Are you aggressively taking steps to pursue that destiny? Or, do you let the circumstances of life choose for you? Goals provide us with purpose and direction. The desire to set goals often begins with the motivation for self-change – to modify some portion of your life. Goals most often represent change, passion, growth, and inspiration. Goals are the avenue for building successful lives.

So often, we focus on achieving tasks, not understanding their meaning or lack of importance to our life's overall goals. Do you have any short-term goals? What are your long-term goals? What do you want to accomplish for your business or personal life? How important is that for you? Where do you see yourself in three years? In five to ten years? What did you do last week to make it happen? What will you do this week to make it happen? What will you do to put yourself one step closer to achieving and accomplishing these goals? What dream do you bury away because you think it isn't practical or you are not deserving of it?

The most powerful way to define direction in your life and your future is to set goals. This can be done by directing your thoughts to attain a specific aim. When you understand exactly what you want and/or need to achieve, you will then know where your efforts should be focused. You must be proactive. You have to take charge and alter your thinking about goals and their connection to your life. This connection will allow your inner beauty to flourish. When you seize control, you will realize that the only way you'll accomplish what you want is to develop your plan and work your plan!

Where Do I Start?

Many high-powered business people, top-level government officials, and high achievers of all walks of life use an established method for setting personal goals. Goal setting involves establishing what you want to achieve, or where you want to go in the short or long-term, and your plan to get there. By setting pointed, well-defined goals, you can measure, and take pride in their achievements. They give you long-term vision and short-term motivation. Once you develop your plan, work it! Always keep in mind that your personal plan is a living document – as your life changes, your plan may need to change also. When you need to, make changes to your plan along the way to keep it up-to-date and relevant.

Exercise

What is your definition of a goal?

1. _____
2. _____
3. _____

Goals should be established in a range of degrees. First, define the ultimate outcome for your life and the major goals you want to achieve. Now, break these down into smaller targets you must hit to obtain your lifetime goal or ultimate life outcome. Once this information has been established, you can then work towards their accomplishment one step at a time.

Consider what you want to do with your life.

Exercise
- What brings you joy?
  _____
  _____

- What are your strengths?
  _____
  _____

- What do you intend to accomplish?
  _____
  _____

- Why is this accomplishment important to you?
  _____
  _____

- What are your limitations?
  _____
  _____

- What are your current accomplishments? Failures?
  _____
  _____

- What are your skills?
  _____
  _____

- What sacrifices are you willing to make?
  _____
  _____

- What values are at the core of your decision?
  _____
  _____

- Does this goal make you feel as though you're making a significant contribution to society?
  _____
  _____

- What deep emotional value or meaning does this have for you?
  _____
  _____

- How do you want others to perceive you?
  _____
  _____

Exercise
1. What is your lifetime goal?
   _____

2. List three long-term goals (10 years):
   - _____
   - _____
   - _____

3. List three short-term goals (1-5 years)
   - _____
   - _____
   - _____

Joy can be found when accomplishing goals. Personal goals often cover many areas in our lives. The list below identifies some areas of life that goals may be applied:

- Attitude – Is there any part of the way you behave that you don't like?

- Career – Are you in the right career for you? Does your current job satisfy you?

- Education – Is there any additional information or skill you want to acquire?

- Financial – Have you established a retirement plan? Would you like to make more money?

- Family – Would you like to have children? Would you like to get married? Do you spend enough time with your loved ones?

- Pleasure – What do you do for fun? Where are you going on vacation this year?

- Spiritual – Are you in touch with your higher power?

Make it real and write it down! List goals for the following:

1. Attitude: _____
2. Career: _____
3. Education: _____
4. Financial: _____
5. Family: _____
6. Pleasure: _____
7. Spiritual: _____

How does this list compare to your lifetime goal? How does this list compare to your list of short and long-term goals? Are these goals that you really want to accomplish, or are they the goals of your family, friends or employer? Do you know and understand who you are? The basis of any plan for your life, or plan for inner development, is based on you truly understanding yourself, and marching to the beat of your own drum. Self-knowledge will assist you in developing realistic and self-satisfying goals.

Putting it Together

Now that you have identified your definition of a goal, as well as identified several of your personal goals, you are now ready to pull together into an achievable design. Review all your goals and create a step-by-step plan to achieve that goal.

Exercise
Select a goal from your short-term or long-term list.
Goal: _____

Strategy for achieving goal:
1. _____
2. _____
3. _____
4. _____

Your next step is to create a daily/weekly to-do list of what must be accomplished to achieve your goal. Your strategy could include: visit museums to broaden cultural understanding, learn to read and/or speak a new language, take a course or training class, begin work on an advanced degree, read the business section from the daily newspaper, attend poetry readings, learn to deep- sea dive or create a business plan. By working out a small detailed written plan, you become focused on how you will achieve your goal. It becomes more realistic! Be certain that your goal and strategies are realistic and attainable. Periodically review your strategies on a weekly and monthly basis to be certain that the strategies are working.

Progress
Working toward your goals will be challenging; therefore, it is important to celebrate achievements every step of the way. Consider a celebration when you achieve a goal. Consider these potential rewards:

- One hour undisturbed bubble bath
- Dinner at your favorite restaurant

- Purchasing those shoes you've been eyeing in Saks' shoe department

- A visit to Victoria's Secret

- Spending the weekend at your favorite Bed and Breakfast

- A weekend fling to Aruba

My favorite reward is a "one hour, do not disturb, burn some candles, turn off the phones, turn on the jazz, and pour me a glass of wine bubble bath". My life is often so hectic that I have limited opportunities to truly take the time to indulge in such pleasure. Don't forget to indulge every once in a while when you have a personal achievement!

Staying Focused

Never take anything for granted. Frequent and precise assessment of your progress is important to the overall effectiveness of your plan. These frequent assessments will help you to truly understand the realities of your situation. You must be ready to adapt your goals and ideas continually. Now that you have achieved this goal (or several goals), think about the following:

- What did you learn from achieving your goal?

- Did you allow enough time to realize the goal?

- Did it take too long to accomplish the goal?

- Could you have done a better job?

- Have you obtained additional information that requires you to add, modify, or remove other goals?

- What, if any, are your new objectives?

- Are your actions in line with your priorities?

Examine questions deeply to get answers. Oftentimes, your goals will change, even if you haven't accomplished or learned anything new. Goals can change with age, time, everyday life changes and/or challenges. You should also note that you might not be able to achieve all of your identified goals. Your failure to meet goals does not constitute personal failure or a failed plan. Use failures or prolonged goal challenges to take decisive action. Look at each obstacle as an opportunity, and every test as a chance to gain knowledge of something new. The people who encounter the most successes are usually those who refuse to let setbacks or rejections hinder them. When challenges abound, discover a new way to meet your goal. Develop a list of lessons learned from the failures, and apply them back to your overall plan accordingly.

Keep your personal goals list in the forefront of your mind. Post it on your desk at work, as part of your to-do list on the refrigerator, or on the nightstand next to your bed. Let the people that know you best, know what you are doing and why. (Keeping family, friends and faith actively in your life will serve as a great stability as you face your goals and potential obstacles.) They can be a great source of support in times of need. Be sure to keep your goals achievable, and don't forget to reward yourself along the way. These rewards will serve as incentives, as well as a form of self-recognition.

Always remember to take consistent and practical actions to accomplish your greatest aspirations. Allow me to be the first to congratulate you!

I'd like to dedicate this chapter to my parents, John P. and Shirley G. Thomas, for laying the foundation for my inner development and growth and to my friend, Dwayne C. Johnson for always encouraging me to pursue my dreams and live my life to the fulliest.

ABOUT THE AUTHOR

KAREN R. DESLANDES

Mrs. DesLandes is the President and Founder of the Institute of Self-Discovery, a personal and professional empowerment organization for women. She is a certified trainer in the areas of diversity & women's issues and wellness for women, and a certified life coach through the Professional Woman Network. She is also a certified human resource manager through Columbia Southern University, as well as a certified trainer/facilitator through Langevin Learning Services for personal & professional development. She has worked in the public sector for over 20 years. Her most recent position is in the Human Resources Department as a Strategic Staffing Recruiter. She is currently an active member of the Professional Woman Network and the National Association for Female Executives. She is Chapter Director of Sister Network NJ, a monthly support group for professional women.

Karen DesLandes places an emphasis on the "Complete Woman". She is passionate about molding women from the inside out. She believes that given the right tools, women can overcome destructive behavior patterns, guilt and shame and become empowered by their pasts and their mistakes, instead of being stopped by them. She has a strong desire to see all women live and thrive in their true purpose. She teaches character development, positive self-image, self-esteem and empowerment, self-acceptance, balance, and the importance of finances and being self-reliant as a means of creating a boundary from the many negative trappings of life.

Mrs. DesLandes is available for seminars, workshops, keynote addresses and personal coaching. She resides with her husband Steven and their four children in Dingmans Ferry, PA.

Contact:
The Institute of Self-Discovery
P.O. Box 154
Dingmans Ferry, PA 18328
(866) 803-7547
selfdisc@ptd.net
www.instituteofselfdiscovery.com

FOUR

THE ART OF FORGIVENESS

By Karen Deslandes

At some point or another, every one of us has had to forgive someone for something they have done to us. We practice this skill almost on a daily basis without even realizing it. When your spouse forgets to save you enough milk for cereal in the morning, you get upset for a moment, but you discuss it and then you move on, right? When another driver cuts you off in traffic, you yell and then you move on. When a co-worker is late handing in their portion of a report, which causes you to also be late, you may be upset for a few days, but eventually you'll discuss what went wrong so that it does not happen again, and then you move on. So, most of us already know how to forgive others in regards to the regular day-to-day issues that life throws our way.

But what about when our feelings and emotions are at stake? Somehow, when our emotions become involved, suddenly all of the rules of the game change. Suddenly, it's not so easy for us to just talk about it, let it go and move on. Why is that? I believe a lot of it has to do with fear, but we will discuss this in a little more detail further on.

Have you ever noticed how, for some people, forgiving seems to come easily, and for others it seems to be a struggle? Have you ever looked at someone that you knew had gone through the unthinkable, yet they didn't seem to show the scars of that trauma? Then you look at others that have a much harder time. When the cashier at the local supermarket is rude to them, they are still holding a grudge the next week when they go back to the supermarket and see the same cashier (as if the cashier has a personal vendetta against them). Are some people just born with a natural ability to forgive, or have they just mastered the secret to living a peaceful life, which is learning to let things go?

So, how do you begin to master the art of forgiving? One of the first things you need to do, as with learning any new skill, is to recognize the significance of acquiring the skill. You must understand the value that learning the skill of forgiveness will add to your life. In order to do that, you must first look at how *not* forgiving is devaluing the quality of your life.

Ask yourself:

1. What are you gaining by holding onto the pain of your past? (i.e.: You get to manipulate others through their guilt over what happened.)

a. _____

b. _____

c. _____

2. What is it costing you by holding onto the pain of your past? (i.e.: Your health because of stress)

a. _____

b. _____

c. _____

It is important for you to understand how crucial it is to process your feelings, because it is the processing that will allow you the ability to forgive. It is a whole lot more complex than simply saying, "My mother was mean to me, so I don't deal with her anymore, and I'm fine with that." Or, "My father left when I was young and I haven't seen him in years, but I'm better off without him." You must allow the full process to run its course. This requires you to get in touch with some painful feelings that you would just as soon forget; otherwise you will find yourself still dealing with the remnants of your past in your current relationships. The decisions you make and the responses you have today will be connected to what has happened in your past if you don't allow true forgiveness to take place.

Even after identifying the importance of forgiveness in your life, understand that it is going to be a learning process, so don't beat yourself up when you don't master it right away. Just as when you are acquiring a new skill or trade, it will be a little uncomfortable when you first start to do it. The same will apply in learning forgiveness, because it will be out of the normal realm of thinking. Most of us react to situations in the manner that society says is normal, yet we wonder why the peace that we are seeking continually eludes us. Yes, it is normal to be angry and upset when someone disappoints you, lies, betrays, or intentionally harms you. But it becomes detrimental to your well-being when you hold onto that anger long after it would be healthy to release it. You should allow yourself to feel the anger because it is normal. Then you should process it by:

- Identifying where the anger is coming from.

- Decide if it's worth it to try to salvage the relationship. If so, communicate where your anger is coming from with the other person.

- If it is not possible to express your anger with the other person, make a commitment to let it go by journaling all of your feelings down, and then promising yourself not to speak of it again, unless it is with a trained professional.

Right now, we will address two areas where non-forgiveness can loom like a dark cloud over your life and keep you stuck in "what happened" instead of freely facing your future.

Forgiving Others

When you haven't allowed yourself to heal from events of your past, it means you are still holding on to non-forgiveness. I think most would agree that forgiveness would be a healthier solution than carrying around a grudge, yet some continue to hold grudges for years against others who have hurt them. So, what stops you from letting go? Let's take a look at some of the things that might keep you from releasing pain from your past that does not serve to bring peace in your life:

- **Fear** – The inability to forgive is based in fear. When someone or something has affected you deeply, you become afraid of opening yourself up and possibly being hurt again, so you continue to hold on to the anger as a means of protecting yourself from more pain.
- **Blame** – Blame makes the situation about the other person. Forgiveness puts the focus back on you so that you can make sure that you are okay. In our society, it seems to be a natural reaction to cast blame. There is always the victim and the villain. When someone harms you in any way, whether it is physically or emotionally, we are quick to point the finger at the perpetrator and demand they be punished. When they are, we feel that the matter has been settled. But what about the victim? Who makes sure that they are okay?
- **The need to be right** – Yes, you probably have a right to be upset with the one who hurt you, but you also have a choice. You can either be right, or you can be free. By letting go, this in no way negates what happened to you, nor does it absolve the person's actions against you, but again, blame keeps you tied to a situation.
- **Denial** – I know that sometimes it seems easier to just live with dysfunction than to take the steps to correct it. We develop mechanisms to make these areas in our lives more bearable, so that they don't hurt as bad. I know it's scary to tread in uncharted territory. And it's not something that will be done overnight. But, at least once you acknowledge the pain, you can begin to take baby steps to begin to overcome it.

Forgiving Yourself

Sometimes even more difficult than forgiving others is being able to forgive yourself. We've all done one thing or another that we would just as soon forget about. You may even wish you had the opportunity to do it all over again. Surely, you would make different choices. Some might still shudder at the very memory of the thing you wish to forget. So how do you begin to forgive yourself?

- **Release the guilt** – Don't allow guilt/condemnation to define who you are. Understand that who you are is not determined by what has happened to you, but how you handle and respond to what has happened. That's the true testament to your character. If you have made strides towards changing whatever behavior has made you feel guilty in the past, understand that's all you can do. You cannot redo the past.
- **Make Restitution** – Is there something you can do to make restitution? If so, take steps towards doing it. If not, you must move on.
- **Learn the Lessons** – Seek what lessons you can learn from the experience. Sometimes you go through experiences that in hindsight you wish you had never allowed to take place, but if you can let go of the anger and guilt, you might find that those very experiences will be a gift you can share with and help others.

Getting to the Root of the Matter

One of biggest keys in learning to forgive and moving on is to get to the heart of what happened so that you can understand and learn from it. Now, I know you are probably saying, "I will never understand *why* they did what they did to me", "I have nothing to learn from the pain they caused me" or "You just don't know what I've done."

If you are not aware of what ails you, how can you address it? It's like going to the doctor's office and not being able to tell him specifically what is bothering you. "I'm just not feeling well" makes it very difficult for the doctor to know how to treat you, or he could treat the wrong ailment, based on the symptoms you tell him. How often we do that in life. We address the symptoms instead of the root of the ailment itself. We will remove ourselves from a situation and feel that all is well. But, life will continuously allow situations to come forward in your life that offer you the opportunity to grow and be made whole. However, if you are not even aware that there is a need for closure, you will not see them as opportunities to learn and grow, but rather as obstacles to go around or avoid. And so the cycle will continue.

Listed below are some examples of how non-forgiveness displays itself.

- *Hypersensitivity to Criticism*

If your supervisor constantly told you that you were not good enough and would never amount to much, you may convince yourself that he is out to get you because he offers constructive criticism about your work. You would take everything as a personal attack against you because you still have unfinished business with those who made you feel inadequate in the past.

- *Unrealistic Expectations of Others*

Perhaps you never felt loved, understood or appreciated by those in your past. Now you are surrounded by those who love you and support you, but to you, it is never enough. You will convince yourself that your husband never has any time for you, your children don't appreciate you, and your friends just don't understand you.

- *Explosive Anger*

Let's say you were bullied as a child, or were picked on by your peers. They might not have heard you or considered your feelings. It left you feeling like no one ever listened to you or cared about how you felt. Now, as an adult, you've become quite the bully yourself. You are determined no one is ever going to treat you that way again. You might have outbursts when you don't feel as if others are hearing you, and you've never made the connection to how you were treated in the past.

- *Self-Hatred*

When you haven't reconciled your past in your mind and heart, you will continue to carry the guilt around. You will gravitate towards situations that are unhealthy, just like the one from your past, because you don't feel that you deserve better.

- *Repeating the Cycle*

If you were abused as a child by those who were supposed to protect you, and you never dealt with your feelings about what happened to you, then you may still carry that anger towards your abusers around with you. You may convince yourself that your own child really is that bad and deserves the degree of discipline that you give him, which really might be severe, but it's all that you understand because you haven't processed your feelings. You will convince yourself that you are the only parent that has a child that misbehaves, and will treat that child with the same harsh treatment that was given to you because you don't have a clear understanding of what went on.

- *Guilt*

Let's say a woman had a baby as a teenager and was made to feel guilty about it by others. Because she accepted and carried the guilt that others put on her, she's never been able to forgive herself. Now, as her own daughter is getting older, she notices she is heading down the same path as she was, but she can't bring herself to talk about it with her daughter because it brings up all of her own feelings of guilt. Instead, she condemns her daughter the same way others condemned her when she was a teenager.

So, how do you move from the anger towards that person to forgiveness? Remember, this is about you being made whole, not about absolving the other person's actions. Following the steps listed below will be helpful to you in moving towards forgiveness.

- **Understanding your own shortcomings helps in forgiving others**. When you are no longer in denial about the areas in your life where you have shortcomings and need forgiveness from others, it helps you to empathize with others who have failed you and more likely to forgive them.
- **Empathy** – Once you are able to understand how or why another person acted towards you in the manner that they did, it gives you insight into the other person's world. It is only then that you begin to realize that, although their actions hurt you, they were not about you, but rather about the other's person's inability to process their own pain.

Affirmations (Repeat these in the mirror everyday until you begin to believe them.)
Forgiving Others What was done to me was not my fault. I did not deserve it. I am a good person worthy of love.
Forgiving Yourself I am not my mistakes. I have learned and grown from them and am worthy of unconditional love.

Exercise:

Answer the following questions about the person that you need to show forgiveness towards.

Who do you need to forgive?

What happened?

How is the pain of that situation still affecting you today?

What steps can you begin to take towards forgiveness?
-
-
-
-

> In what ways would your life improve if you were to forgive this person?
> -
> -
> -
> -

Look at those areas in your life where you know you overreact or take things to the extreme. Perhaps someone does something to you or says something to you, and you feel your blood start to boil. Maybe you find yourself in a situation that feels all too familiar, and it takes you back to that area of your life that is incomplete. Whatever the situation, before you react, ask yourself this: In all honesty, can you say that you are totally present in the moment, or are you blending unresolved feelings from your past with this situation? If so, take some time before you react until you can be sure that you are only dealing with your present situation. I know that it's easier said than done, but once you have become aware of what is unfinished in your life, you owe it to yourself and those in your life to have closure with the events from your past so that you can be fully present to experience all that your life has to offer today.

Forgiveness puts you in the position to overcome your past, which can be a daunting responsibility, because it now means that you are responsible for your life and choices. However, with that responsibility also comes the freedom to make more positives choices, and to design your life the way you truly desire.

ABOUT THE AUTHOR

RIKI F. LOVEJOY-BLAYLOCK

Riki F. Lovejoy-Blaylock, is a returning author in the PWN Series, having completed her works in *Becoming the Professional Woman, The SuperWoman Syndrome, Women's Survival Guide for Overcoming Obstacles, Transition & Change* and her latest, *Women As Leaders: Strategies for Empowerment & Communication*. Her experiences as a business owner in the male-dominated construction industry afford her the ability to talk from the heart about *Embracing Fears*. Entering the construction industry in 1985 as a receptionist, Riki knew early on she wanted to be at the top some day and she knew this could not be accomplished without facing and overcoming her fears. It took over 20 years but Riki fully understands the positive effects of her life today were due to the challenges accepted along the way.

Riki has worked for major general contractors in the Orlando, Florida market as a Project Manager and owned a carpentry subcontracting company in the early 90's. Currently Riki is the Executive Director for *RFL Consulting Solutions, LLC*, a construction management consulting firm, with management contracts on projects throughout the country. Her career has taken her to other parts of the world including BeiJing, People's Republic of China, Europe and the Caribbean.

Riki is a certified Minority Business Enterprise through the Florida Minority Suppliers Development Council as well as a certified Woman's Business Enterprise through the National Women Business Owners Corporation. Riki is continuously named to the Cambridge Who's Who of Business and Professional Executives and most recently was elected as the Region 3 (State of Florida) Director for the National Association of Women In Construction.

Contact:
Riki F. Lovejoy, Executive Director
RFL Consulting Solutions, LLC
5607 Bay Side Drive
Orlando, FL 32819-4046
Office: 407.443.3423
Fax: 407.612.6300
Email: rlovejoy@rfl-consulting.com

FIVE

EMBRACING FEAR

By Riki Lovejoy Blaylock

"You gain strength, courage, and confidence by every experience in which you really stop to look fear in the face. You are able to say to yourself, 'I lived through this horror. I can take the next thing that comes along."
—Eleanor Roosevelt

If, by now, you have become a fan of the PWN Library and its series of books, you have already read about *Overcoming Fear*, by Sharyn Yonkman in **Becoming the Professional Woman** and *Face Your Fear!* by Elizabeth Palm in **Women's Survival Guide for Overcoming Obstacles, Transition & Change**. Both of these fellow authors take you through the journey of figuring out what fears are hindering your personal and professional successes, and then provide methods of facing these fears to overcome the roadblocks to your success. They really have said it all, given you all the exercises that you could use, and provided a lot of food for thought. So why am I writing about essentially the same topic, you may be asking? Because I'm going to reiterate to you one of the main themes in Sharyn's and Liz's chapters – fear can be good for you. Embrace it and you will become more empowered!

Fear is a fact of life that we cannot escape. Oh sure, you may be one of those people that says, "I'm not afraid of anything!" But guess what – the biggest fear you have is probably that you are afraid of something! Fear is our own worst enemy; it strongholds us into not moving forward, and keeps us frozen in our tracks. Let's face it, we've all learned by now that self-esteem and fear play off of each other – the higher your fear level the lower your self-esteem, and vice versa! You know that when you have faced your fear and are victorious, your self-esteem jumped up a notch or two, or ten! It's all starting to make sense, isn't it?

So, fear is here to stay. What can we do with it? Sharyn and Liz say – face it and overcome it! I'm adding *embrace it*! Use the fear to propel you forward to becoming a fearless individual that, as Mrs. Roosevelt said, can take on anything.

Know Who The Enemy Is!

I love Dictionary.com! They have the typical definitions, and then I find definitions that make me think a little more. So "fear" is defined as we would typically think – "a distressing emotion aroused by impending danger, evil, pain, etc., whether the threat is real or imagined; the feeling or condition of being afraid." The definition that really makes me think, hmmmmm, is "a reverential awe, especially towards God." Let's think about this… a fear or being in awe of something good, of something powerful, of something that could make a huge difference in our lives! Yep, I think that's the definition we are talking about here! But we have to understand the essentialness of fear – it is an emotion. Emotion is not the enemy.

Whaaatt! Not the enemy!? Okay, now you're asking, where the heck is she trying to go with this? Sharyn says fear is not the problem, but how we *deal with* the fear! Now we're getting somewhere. The problem is how we deal with the fear, when we run or when we face the fear, when we overcome the fear, or when we totally give in to it, which believe it or not is a viable option. The problem is not the enemy.

Okay, before I totally lose you, I'll give you a hint. Look in the mirror. The enemy is us!

Oooohh, didn't like to hear that, did you? Dealing with fear, just like fear itself, is a fact of life, for we cannot live our lives in fear of everything. Sure, sure, there are some fears that may not necessarily be a problem to have, and that viable option we mentioned earlier of doing nothing is okay, like the fear of snakes (the squirmy ones – not the smooth talkers!) and you live in New York City. It's not likely that you will have to face many snakes in NYC. Of course, if you live in Florida and little black snakes are prevalent in your garden, then you may need to face the fear, and learn a method of 'coping' with the fear. This is a fear that will never go away!

But there are fears that are holding you back from being the consummate professional that you know you can or want to be. Fear of networking, fear of being asked a question that you don't immediately know the answer, fear of public speaking, fear of co-authoring a series of books with an incredible group of other women! How would you face and overcome these fears? Or will you? Will you face and overcome, or will you do nothing? Will you be your own worst enemy?

By embracing the fear you have, you are acknowledging its existence. And if you've been doing all of your exercises that Sharyn and Liz have walked you through, you have the tools to move forward to your successes and you have already started your journey to a higher level of self-esteem. You are already learning to conquer the enemy!

The Plan of Attack – Conquering the Enemy!

This gets so confusing, really. You don't really want to conquer you, but you do want to conquer the you that gives in to your fear! Can you see what I mean? Of course, the first object of the plan of attack (after knowing who the enemy is) is understanding the fears you have, and why. Is your fear of snakes because you were attacked by a snake as a child? Or is it a fear because everyone else says it is? Is the fear real? What is your fear of networking all about? And just what is all this talk about the fear of public speaking? Have you actually done it more than once? If so, you must have survived! And, you added that 'notch' in your self-esteem yardstick. Let's do one of the exercises, again! Maybe today your fear list is different than when you compiled a year ago.

Fears That Are Holding You Back Professionally	How REAL Are These Fears?
[Example: Networking]	Very
1.	
2.	
3.	
4.	

If the fears made it to this list, you probably also said the fears are real. Let's examine how real they really are by examining the reason for the fear – remember the snake example from earlier.

Why Is The Fear Real?
[Example: Because no one likes to do it, and I consider myself a shy person.]
1.
2.
3.
4.

Now, let's examine the "Example" answer. How real is this? "No one likes to do it" is more of a perceived fear and you are just going with the flow. The "…consider myself a shy person" could have some validity to it, but should not be a part of the 'fear factor'.

Next, let's look to see if there are any real life situations currently going on in your career that you could specifically use to address your plan of attack. For instance, is there a trade association event or meeting that you could go to (and for the sake of this learning process, go alone!) that would afford you an opportunity to network for your company.

List An EVENT or TASK that Addresses the Fear You Showed Above.
[Example: ABC Trade Association is meeting Tuesday night at 5:30 p.m.]
1.
2.
3.
4.

Have you realized anything at this point? Have you <u>really</u> looked at your list of fears that are holding you back professionally? If the list is a typical list, it included in some form or fashion: networking, public speaking, being asked to perform a task for which you feel you are not qualified, or have to learn that new software program being implemented. Although, in our minds, these are very important fears, fears that truly do hold us back from moving forward in our careers, they are just not very REAL fears. They have become fears that have been learned through societal inputs, or even those naysayers or individuals who have unconsciously taught you these fears. By facing and overcoming these fears (and probably more importantly the origin of these fears) you have opened your mind to the possibilities of all!

Okay, so let's do one last exercise to finish off our plan of attack. This one sets goals for the event or task that you have chosen to work through your respective fears.

What Do I Want To Accomplish When I Face The Fear Through This Event or Task?
[Example: I Will Meet Seven New People and Exchange Business Cards Regardless of Their Business and Whether I Need Their Service or Product.]
1.
2.
3.
4.

The goal becomes the focus of the event rather than the fear of participating in the event being the focus. Plus, by planning your goals for each of your events or tasks tools that you choose to use to face and overcome your fear, you have a better realization of the underlying meaning of your fear. When you walk away from the event with a success notch, you realize that maybe your fear was / is unwarranted. The next time you do something outside of your comfort zone, you won't have the same 'freak-out' because you know you can do anything!

This Attack is Over – But the Battle Goes On…

When you walk away from the event or task you have outlined here, you could have a myriad of emotions, because the truth of the matter is that you will seemingly fail at some of the tasks you will try. But you haven't really failed because you did the most important thing – you **embraced the fear**, you overcame the fear, and most importantly – you did something! Now you can embrace fear because you have learned that every failure is actually a lesson. And what do you suppose the lesson is? The lesson is that you can … DO … Anything! And that if the TASK is a failure, you are still okay, and more empowered to move on to the next task!

The Litany Against Fear
I must not fear.
Fear is the mind-killer.
Fear is the little-death that brings total obliteration.
I will face my fear.
I will permit it to pass over me and through me.
And when it has gone past, I will turn the inner eye to see its path.

> *Where the fear has gone, there will be nothing.*
> *Only I will remain.*
> —Frank Herbert

A theory, which may be hard to grasp with this whole embracing fear concept, is that you have to experience failure, and then move forward. If you do not embrace the fear, you end up staying in your comfort zone. If you do not experience failure, you do not learn what to do different or better. It becomes a vicious circle, because when we fail, we tend to withdraw, returning back to the comfort zone. You cannot do this! And think about this, some of the greatest successes of our time – Velcro®, Post-It® Notes and even some vaccines – were mistakes or considered as failures.

I am not advocating you to jump off a bridge because you have a fear of heights, or race around a racetrack on a horse because speed frightens you to no end. There is a purpose for the emotion of fear, and that is to protect you from the real dangers. But these types of dangers are a different level than what we are addressing in this Chapter. What I encourage you to do is step out on a limb for just one of your fears. Yes, I had you do an exercise where you listed multiple fears, but if you are new to the notion of embracing fear, don't add another fear to the list – the fear of being afraid to try!

Fear often takes on other faces or emotions – anger, addiction, or depression. You need to recognize fear in its truest form. So how can you do this? And why would you want to? Again, we find that fear and these other emotions feed off each other, much like we mentioned earlier about self-esteem. The fear you may have had from an early age may today manifest itself into anger or depression. So, unless you understand where the emotions, including fear, come from, you will not be able to move forward. And let me complicate this a little more – what is the difference between fears and phobias? As defined earlier in this Chapter, fear is a reaction to a threat – real or perceived. Phobia is like a fear gone wild. You cannot walk into a room of strangers because of your intense fear of networking. So you have fear, anger, depression, phobias – what DO you DO?

You continue to confront your fear. Just like when we started your exercises earlier, I mentioned that your fear today may be different than what you may have had a year ago when you started your self-improvement journey with the PWN Series books (or any other self-help method you may be using!). The battle of overcoming fears will be an on-going battle, but the more you practice, the better you get, and the easier it becomes. You can destroy your fears, lose the anger and depression, and most likely the phobias, by continually chipping away. And just because you face your fear the first time does not mean the fear goes away instantly. You have to keep at it to annihilate the original fear. Just like our example, don't go to just the one Trade Association event and think you are cured. Keep on going; each time you go will be easier than the time before, until one day networking is no longer a fear, but a way of life as you move forward in your business.

Embracing Your Fear is the first step to overcoming your fear! Overcoming Your Fear will be an exciting journey if you keep at it. But remember that Life isn't about reaching a goal – Life Is The Journey! And the rewards you receive along the way – physically, emotionally and maybe even monetarily – will make it all worthwhile. Enjoy the fear!

You never know until you try.
And you never try unless you <u>really</u> try.

You give it your best shot;
You do the best you can.

And if you've done everything in your power, and still "fail" –
The truth of the matter is
That you haven't failed at all.

When you reach for your dreams, no matter what they may be,
You grow from the reaching;
You learn from the trying;
You win from the doing.
—Laine Parsons

Notes:

ABOUT THE AUTHOR

Patricia A. Cheeseboro

Patricia A. Cheeseboro is the President and CEO of Cheeseboro Consulting Services, which is dedicated to inspiring and motivating professional and personal growth in individuals and organizations through workshops, seminars and whole-life coaching.

Patricia has worked for over sixteen years as a caseworker with the Commonwealth of Pennsylvania Department of Public Welfare, and has a strong background in case management, counseling, and writing individual plans for self-sufficiency. Ms. Cheeseboro earned a Bachelor of Science degree from Pennsylvania State University in Individual and Family Studies, in 1980. She is a Certified Consultant and Trainer with The Professional Woman Network (PWN), specializing in Professional Development and Youth Issues.

She is the wife of Andrew Cheeseboro and the mother of three daughters — Jasmine, Amber, and Nia. She is inspired by her family members who allow her to pursue her passion in helping others.

Patricia has a passion for training and motivating others to be empowered and to realize their full potential in spite of their circumstances. Here motto is "I can do all things through Christ who strengthens me." (Philippians 4:13) Patricia is a highly=capable consultant and inspiring speaker, providing services both nationally and internationally.

Contact
Cheeseboro Consulting Services
P.O. Box 15586
Pittsburgh, PA 15244
(412) 965-0418
PACheeseboro@aol.co
www.protrain.net

SIX

YOUR LEGACY: WHAT WILL YOU LEAVE FOR OTHERS?

By Patricia Cheeseboro

The definition of a legacy is something special that one leaves behind to be remembered by, and the contributions they make that give value and meaning to their life. Legacy, as defined by Webster: "1. Something received from an ancestor or predecessor or from the past. 2. How someone is remembered and what contributions they made while they lived." Many people think of a legacy as monetary bequest. But a legacy that is more valuable, and something money can't buy, is one that is driven by your purpose for being, based on you values and passion or matters of the heart. Each day that we live and breathe we are living our legacy. Our journey through life is our living legacy; whether unconsciously or by design, we live how we are going to be remembered.

Are You Living Your Legacy Unconsciously, or By Design?

If your answer is "**unconsciously**", then it will mean that you have no goals, dreams or vision for your life. Or could mean that you are living on hurts, broken promises or shattered dreams? You may be allowing your negatives attributes to take control of your attitudes and thoughts, and thus effect how you treat others. If you answered **"by design"** then you are living your legacy with definite goals and plans. You are inspired to be mindful and proactive in your actions, thoughts and life. A designed legacy has established that there is a purpose for its being, and has an aspiration to leave a trace of the legacy behind.

Your life purpose is the essence of who you are as a person, and it is the fundamental to living your legacy for several reasons:

- It gives you a sense of fulfillment and meaning as to why you were born.

- It allows you to use your values and passion, and directs them towards a meaningful goal.

- It motivates and drives you to achieve, as well as deposit into others.

- It brings out your own uniqueness of who you are, and brings out your special gifts, talents, and abilities to shape the world you want to live in, and to leave for your children and your children's children.

- You realize that adversities are not stumbling blocks but stepping stones, and often valuable lessons that make you stronger in your journey through life.

- It gives you focus on a primary message for your life.
- It has no impact if it only involves you; your purpose has to include others, or it has no impact.

Your purpose is most powerfully expressed not by **what** you do, but by **who** you are and the legacy you leave behind.

Why Is It Important to Live and Create a Legacy?

It can be empowering to know that you have a voice and control of how you live your life, and how you will be remembered. A well-designed legacy is powerful and thought provoking, because it pulls you forward to make a difference in your life and others. It provides the course for positive, long term changes, and provides an opportunity to make a lasting impact on many levels beyond your lifetime.

How Do You Begin to Design the Legacy?

So you want to start living your legacy. How do you start? It begins with you taking an inventory of your life, and then producing a life resume with a life mission statement. To start, you need to establish some quiet time for yourself and reflect upon your life. Before you begin this reality check, light some candles, put on some light smooth instrumental music, only jazz or classical, take a long luxury bath and reflect on you. Then curl up in you favor chair. Write in your journal, "What is the legacy *I* want to create?" *"I"* is the operative word because it is all about *you*. This is your life story and you are the star "reality" actress. Write the following:

1. List **Your Core Values.** What drives your world? (i.e. love, trust, honesty, friendship)

    - _____
    - _____
    - _____
    - _____

2. What is **Your Passion in Life?**

    - _____
    - _____
    - _____

3. What are **Your Most Important Accomplishments to Date?**

    - _____
    - _____
    - _____

4. **What is Your Vision for Your Life Legacy?** Try answering these questions:

    - What would I like to change or improve for my family, in my community (or even globally)?

        _____

- What would I want to be remembered for?

  _____

- What will I have to do have to commit to in order to produce the type of legacy I will need to live and/or leave?

  _____

5. With all the information you have based on your core values passion statement, write your mission statement as the core objective of your legacy. Include the action plan and who are the supporting people or systems to help me to create your legacy.

Mission Statement

_____
_____
_____
_____

Action Plan Check-List		
What I Need to Accomplish	Who Can Help	Completion Date

This exercise is a true reality check, and when you finish it should be a blueprint for living your legacy. Read over what you have written. Does the thought of a legacy overwhelm you or empower you? Leaving a legacy should empower you, because it draws out the greatness in you and allows your authentic self to shine. If you are overwhelmed, then you are either setting unrealistic goals that you will struggle with from day to day, or you are afraid that you are going to fall short in living your legacy. Set realistic goals, surround yourself with people who can make your legacy come true, and set your action plan into motion.

A Matter of the Heart is Our Richest Legacy

Once you have established your purpose and determine your life mission statement based upon your core values and passions, you are on your way to living your legacy. (Of course, you may still have to give yourself a reality check from time to time. Even with all the designing and planning, you may still miss the mark.) However, if you focus on matters of the heart, you will always be able to put yourself back on track, as you understand the priceless inheritance of what matters most: A heart-driven legacy.

Ways to Live the Legacy

• The words of encouragement or kind gesture to a stranger who may cross your path for a brief moment can change your life. Think about strangers who were placed in your path while you were feeling low, and they gave you words of encouragement without ever knowing that they made a difference.

- Create special memories with your children; attend their school activities, walk in the park, share quiet time, or share popcorn and watch a movie together. Create special times with your spouse and other people in your life. (My husband, Andrew has started a ritual of date night once a month. These dates are even better than when we were courting, and more memorable!)

- Tell family stories and keep your ancestors' memories alive; reveal the inheritance that was left to remind you that, "We wear the mask of our Ancestors." In 2006, this was the theme chosen for my family reunion by the planning committee of young people. My daughter wrote a poem titled, "We wear the mask of our Ancestors", and she gave all the core values of our forefathers who gave us the inherited legacy of compassion, love, faith, integrity, the gift of humor, sacrifices, a deep love for family, and living a purpose driven life based upon the principles of God. These principles are the inherited gifts my ancestors gave to me, and as I grow older, these gifts are more precious than if they had left me diamonds and gold. (Yes, most of us would rather have the diamonds and gold, but the truth of the matter is, most of us do not come from wealthy families. My ancestors' gifts are the foundation for my own living legacy, and my purpose and vision for life.)

- Tell your life stories, including your mistakes you made along the way, to help others from making the same mistakes. Oftentimes we don't share our mistakes, but if we do let others know problems of the past, we might even stop generational curses.

- Remind your loved ones each day that you love them. (My brother is BIG on this, as nine out of ten times when he ends a telephone call, he says, "I love you.") Love is the most powerful gift you can give anyone.
- Thank others who have helped you get where you are today, and then reach back and help someone else. The most valuable part of purpose is helping others, and providing a gift for generations to come.
- Mentor someone. Share your life story both good and bad, your beliefs about events that happened in your life, why you feel way you do, and how it affected you. (My husband was mentoring a young man who has become part of our family and has been battling with cancer. Blake has given us all courage from his wisdom. He is living his legacy.)
- Share your joys in your life and things that made who you are, such as the love of music or the writing of poetry.
- If you have an heirloom, explain why it is important and why you are handing it down to the person you are giving it to. In the movie "Down in the Delta", the family heirloom was a silver candelabra named "Nat", which dated back to the Civil War. The great great-great grandfather had taken it from the home of the slave master who had obtained it for the sale of his father. It was about hope, sacrifice and the importance of love and family. Think about your ancestors' legacy and what inheritance you received from your ancestors. Make sure that their legacy continues on through each generation. We are entrusted with their cherished legacy through life stories, and sometimes even material inheritance. Share with your family the struggles, challenges, and journeys that your late family members encountered. Individual stories will become unique legacies for future generations, provide

encouragement for overcoming personal challenges, and help others to rise up when they have fallen.

When It Is All Said And Done

At the age of sixteen, I had to write my own obituary as part of a Sunday school assignment. I can still remember the awkward feeling as I completed the assignment in third person. To further intensify my feelings, I had to read it out loud. Hearing it brought a lot of mixed emotions and a reality check. The assignment bothered me because I couldn't imagine my own death! I had not even begun to live and I feared death! It was a reality check! The reality was that someday my life would end, and I wanted my "reality" obituary to be one that was filled with accomplishments. I wanted my life to have made a difference.

To think about your own mortality can make you start living a more purpose driven life. It will keep you focused and help you set priorities. It will help direct your goals and plan how you want to be remembered. Not one of us knows how long we will be on Earth, but striving to live a life of legacy **each day** as if it were our last will assure us that the legacy we leave will be one of the heart.

What will you leave behind? Some of us would like to stop world hunger, find a cure for cancer, leave a hefty endowment or write a *book.* The women of PWN, who are all part of the PWN Library, are leaving a legacy through their chapters and the lives we are touching through our business and families. Believe it or not, your legacy began long before you were ever born. We inherit gifts that come from everyone who has touched our lives and left an impact through our ancestors, parents, siblings, family and friends, teachers, spiritual leaders, co-workers and sometimes complete strangers. We are all here for a purpose, and we all will leave a legacy behind.

My Legacy

This morning I awoke and the sun was shining brightly, but the air was silent and sweet.
I told everyone good morning as I entered the room,
but no one seemed to respond.
Their faces seemed solemn and filled with pain, and
some were glistening with tears.
I asked what was wrong, and they all looked at the picture on the wall.
I couldn't see, so I moved closer to take a look.
But suddenly the door opened, and everyone turned as if expecting
someone else to enter.
I saw their faces turned to disappointment
as they glanced at the picture once more.
The person told them it was time and they all left the room.
I froze for a moment, as the picture was me, and
hurried to catch up with them.
I embraced each of my children and whispered softly to them.
I love you always, and I have left each of you a special part of me.
I placed my hand over their heart so the warmth of my love could be felt.
Jasmine, I gave you my compassion for others, and love for life.
Amber, I gave you my creativity, and the love of travel and independence.
Nia, I gave you my sensitivity and creativity, and the love of knowledge.
Hold true to the sweet memories and share them for generations to come.
You know of my struggles and sacrifices.
You know of my faith in God, and that my prayers
will continue to cover you.
You know that you are loved by me, always and forever.
I looked and saw someone beckon me on.
I turned to leave, and watched matters of my heart be disposed into each.

And as they each smiled,
I knew that my legacy would be told to generations to come.
I blew a sweet kiss to my precious, little angels, Maya, Ayana and Saniya.
They would tell my legacy for future generations.
Traces of me will remain forever.
—Patricia Cheeseboro

ABOUT THE AUTHOR

TAMERA SWAN MASON

Tamera Swan Mason has always been a multifaceted individual who wears many hats. She is currently the Administrator and occasional lecturer for the Unity Center of Christianity in Baltimore, Maryland, a non-denominational New Thought organization. Educationally, she holds a Master of Public Administration degree from the University of Baltimore, and is currently studying with the University of Metaphysics in conjunction with the University of Sedona. She will receive her Master of Science in Metaphysics in 2008, specializing in metaphysical counseling and training. As a certified trainer and member of the Professional Woman Network, Tamera has combined her knowledge of diversity and women's issues with metaphysics in assisting her to enhance her counseling activities.

She has authored two books; *How to Start And Operate a Home-Based Business* and *Mail Order Mania*. She offers her services as a workshop facilitator in the areas of Board Leadership Training and Small Business Management. She presently contributes as an adjunct professor, teaching business subjects at a local college.

Five years ago she started a mail order company called White Swan by promoting her own line of personal care products for women. Her products are known as "Wild Rose" because of their unique rose fragrance.

Tamera advises women to follow their dreams. There are many challenges that women face in life that will take them away from their timetable of accomplishment. But the women who ultimately succeed are the women who continue to strive and <u>never give up</u> no matter how long it takes their dreams to come to fruition.

Contact:
Tamera Swan Mason
White Swan
PO Box 303
Randallstown, MD 21133
www.metamorphosis10@comcast.net
www.whiteswanproducts.com
(410) 521-4249

SEVEN

MIRROR, MIRROR: LOOK INSIDE

By Tamera Swan Mason

When I was a child, my parents read me many interesting and thought provoking fairy tales. Many of these fairy tales had a theme that, unfortunately, many children could not always understand. One of the fairy tales I remember that I liked very much was Snow White and the Seven Dwarfs. I became particularly fascinated each time the wicked witch looked in the mirror and was outraged because the mirror did not tell her what she wanted to know.

When you look into the mirror each morning, what do you see? Is it the warm, loving, kind individual that God made you to be, or are you constantly seeing all the things you don't like about yourself? Your nose is too big, your lips are too small or too broad, your hair doesn't hold curl, your face has a funny shape, big hips or no hips, you want clear radiant skin like you used to have when you were young, etc., etc.

The Sky is the Limit.

As women, we do ourselves a disservice by not acknowledging the great human beings we really are. We are all constructed with different bodies, personalities, abilities and talents. We have different perspectives on life and living. But for some reason, many women still find themselves very inferior, not only to their male counterparts, but to other women, as well. Fifty years ago many women simply did not aspire to cultivate their talents to the extent they do today.

We are proud to have many women in "high places" doing fantastic jobs at whatever they do. Today the sky is the limit, and we must learn to see our greatness as individuals and do all we can to promote ourselves, both as individuals and as a group.

Begin to See the Real You!

What we often see in that mirror are the lines of time and the gray hair beginning to protrude. We are quick to judge ourselves unfairly, according to what we feel are our many faults. After a period of time, as we look into that mirror we wonder where the time has gone, and we think about all the things we missed or could have done differently. Boy! Does that mirror play havoc with our lives! We love to talk about our ailments, our doctor's appointments, our disabilities, the cost of our prescriptions, and we describe them in great detail.

Suppose the next time you look into that mirror you see a vibrant, intelligent, attractive woman designed for greatness; ready to make wonderful changes in the world by simply being yourself.

Keep a Daily Journal.

In the evening before going to bed, make a practice of looking into the mirror and making a list of all the good things you see about yourself: your talents, abilities, accomplishments, dreams and goals. Consider just how far you have come in reaching those goals, no matter how little has been accomplished. Think about what you did today that helped someone else. Whose heart did you warm today with a cheerful hello and a pleasant smile? We never realize just how we affect others. Would your family be as healthy and as comfortable if you were not there to take care of them? Women know how to provide encouragement and support for their children and spouses, but often fail to see themselves as recipients of their own worthiness.

Keep this journal on your dresser or night stand and write these things down. By acknowledging these simple little tasks, you will be surprised at how your self- confidence will increase, and how you will begin to feel good about yourself. As you take a good look at the personality that stares back at you in the mirror, be aware that you are a unique and creative individual with much to give the world. See yourself as the individual you **REALLY** are, and begin to be thankful for your many talents and abilities. Give thanks always for being you, and you will be surprised at how well and how quickly you will allow the **REAL** you to appear. The more you realize who and what you really are, the more you will be inspired to cash in on bringing forth more of that wonderful person.

Pat Yourself on the Back!

As you begin to look at yourself, remember that you are a multifaceted individual. What you see in the mirror is only the surface material, the packaging that you came "wrapped in". Look at yourself from a psychological, spiritual, and emotional standpoint, as well as your physical makeup. Remember, real beauty is not measured by the amount of makeup or fancy clothes we wear, but by the amount of uplifting we give. So, give yourself a pat on the back and uplift your own soul to another level.

See Yourself in a New Light.

Think of this practice as a three-month process. Maintain the practice of writing in your journal for at least a month. After a month, discontinue writing in your journal. During the third month, go back to your journal and re-read it to discover if any progress has been made concerning how you feel about yourself. Have you started a new hobby that has always interested you? Has your attitude changed about many of the negative factors that you were previously holding? Do you see yourself in a new light? Are you a more understanding, giving, and forgiving individual? What would really make you happy at this time in your life? If the answer to these questions is positive and you feel really good about yourself, then you are on your way to opening up a whole new avenue of life. If your answer is not positive, then you need to return to writing in your journal and exploring who and what you really are. By continuing to delve deeply into your consciousness, you will discover the real you. For some, it may take more work than for others. But however long it takes, you owe it to yourself to get to the core of the real you and bring that individual into your outer world.

Where Do Your Real Talents Lie?

I'm sure you have noticed how some people do certain things so well, and others have no talent whatsoever in that particular area. We all have a specific place and purpose in this world, as indicated by our talents and attributes, each one different from the other, but so often, for one reason or another, we allow our talents to lie dormant because of our inability to really see what lies beneath the surface.

Let's begin to work diligently to discover and cultivate these talents. I love to bake. While this does not seem to be an earth-shattering talent, I get a great deal of satisfaction in being able to make a good tasting loaf of bread. I am also pleased when my family enjoys it. For some, this may be an undesirable chore that they would not want to handle. But this is a part of who and what I am.

It's up to you to discover all the facets of your makeup and take full advantage of who and what you really are. Enjoy being you without any criticism or second thoughts about what you could be.

When I was in school, we took a series of personality and aptitude tests. These tests were supposed to reveal our true likes and dislikes, and the areas in which we would do well and steer us in the right direction for employment. However, many of us eventually found ourselves in unhappy positions in the workforce. We did not take these tests seriously enough to follow their advice. Thus again, those attributes that were unique to each of us were not pursued. Many of us find ourselves changing careers in mid-stream. We live longer, enjoy good health, and as a result, we are in the work force much longer. These tests might still be an avenue that we could consider as another method of looking beneath the surface to discover a great deal more about ourselves. But, fear not, it is not too late. There are independent companies that provide aptitude tests to anyone who is interested. If you would like to have professional help in this area, consider availing yourself of this service.

Is God a Part of Your Life?

For those of you who are religious individuals, you know that you are children of a loving God who has endowed you with the talents and abilities to carry out his will and honor him on this Earth. Failing to utilize all that God has given you is denying God's will. We are but a very tiny part of God's creation, but a very important part, each of us with a specific role to play or task to fulfill. One of the Bible verses that I like very much says, "Let your light so shine before men that they may see your good works, and glorify your father that is in heaven."

Have you discovered your role yet? Are you playing your part? Many of us go through life selling ourselves short, never really understanding who we are. If we only realized how precious we are, how important we are, how much God depends on each and every one of us to do his perfect work, we would be far happier than we are. What a wonderful awakening this would be for so many of us. Many of us have endeavored to discover ourselves spiritually.

If you would like to seek help in discovering yourself spiritually, seek counseling from the many counselors that specialize in expanding the spiritual consciousness to allow you to see yourself from this viewpoint.

Unlike the wicked witch in the fairy tale, the mirror that we place so much value upon is only an instrument for us to view our greatness, not our faults. Greatness that comes from within!

The Real Personality Takes Over!

As you begin to work with yourself, you will find that the real personality takes over with the greatest of ease. How many times have you seen an unattractive woman who exudes so much personality, excitement, or dedication that you forgot what she really looks like? Her personality takes over and you see the real person. This individual understands her greatness, despite the many faults she may feel she has. She has acquired real confidence in herself, and she is able to look past the surface and see her inner self. This is extremely important because then and only then can she concentrate on becoming more of what she really is without being concerned about the outer framework.

When I think of great women who fall in this category who gave much to the world, I think of Mother Theresa and Eleanor Roosevelt, women of great courage and fortitude who strived to make a difference. These are just two of the many women who understood their talents and abilities, and took it upon themselves to give all they could.

There are many avenues we can take to truly discover all aspects of ourselves. It is extremely important that we do not allow ourselves to become depressed and overwrought by the lack of self-confidence and self-acceptance.

By seeing the real you, all those magnificent inner qualities, and experiencing this new self-knowledge, it will open many doors for you that have thus far been closed. There is no one else like you and there will never be anyone else like you.

As human beings, we are constantly involved in a process of change; our bodies change, our personalities change, our goals and aspirations change. But this change also presents us with new life, new avenues to explore, and the ability to take advantage of new opportunities. It can be exciting, and we should view it as a constant adventure. But one thing that should never change is the way in which we see ourselves; loving, kind, exciting, intelligent, vibrant women with a great deal to give to the world. This is what we should see every time we look into our mirror.

Recommended Reading

Liberating Your Magnificence by Shannon & Scott Peck; Lifepath Publishing, 1999

Encouraging Words for Women by Darlene Sala; Barbour Publishing, Inc., 2002

Notes:

ABOUT THE AUTHOR

L. Denise Jackson

L. Denise Jackson, a certified counselor, speaker, and trainer, business development consultant, and a published writer, received her academic education from American University and University of Maryland. As she continues her studies towards becoming a certified counselor through American Association of Christian Counselors, she currently holds personal development retreats. She speaks, counsels, and trains many women (and some men) at local and regional conferences, consults clients nationally, and conducts the *Leave Your Baggage Behind...It's Time to Move On!* several times during the year. A New Jersey Native residing in Washington, DC, she enjoys reading, traveling, and spending time with family and friends.

Contact:
L. Denise Jackson,
611 Pennsylvania Avenue, SE, #383
Washington, DC 20003
202-397-4515
womenforsuccess_dc@yahoo.com
www.seminarsforyou.citymax.com

EIGHT

AVOIDING TOXIC RELATIONSHIPS

By L. Denise Jackson

If you are in a toxic relationship, RUN! Cut the ties and just RUN! Do not look back, just RUN!

This could be the shortest chapter in this book if everyone fully understood what a toxic relationship entails and how to get out. With many, that is not the case. So, let's get started to set you free from a relationship (or relationships) that are not healthy, helpful, or supportive of your full greatness.

Relationships

Toxic relationships can be with a friend, co-worker, business partner, family member, romantic interest, or personal or business associates whom you interact with or see occasionally or frequently. You may be casually connected or have a very close, intimate relationship with the person. To reach the majority of this books readers, we will examine close relationships—people you interact with daily or weekly.

What is a Toxic Relationship?

Think of a toxic relationship like a toxic spill. The effects are very similar. Toxic spills are detrimental to the environment and destroy whatever life that exists. The affected life is poisoned by being overtaken by the toxin (a substance that accumulates in the body and causes it harm), and will soon cease existence or scarcely survive. This is similar to what happens when you are in a toxic relationship. You are the life and the person you are in a relationship with is the toxin. The most important difference between a toxic spill and a toxic relationship is that you have the power to overcome and survive the toxicity of the poisonous relationship.

Toxic relationships cause stress, which can elevate into tragedy. What does that mean to you? How do you know if you are in a toxic relationship? Are your needs not being met. Are your constantly struggling for affection, attention, encouragement, love and support? Are you looking for the other person to fill your expectations and reassure you that everything will be okay? Does your interaction with the other person result in more bad days than good? Do you feel drained with the thought of seeing this person or spending any time with them? Are you filled with dread when you anticipate what will happen or be said? Do they always have something negative to say and fail to uplift you even when they say they are trying? Do they reject things you do from your heart or not acknowledge them at all? Do you often feel injured emotionally, spiritually, or physically by the person? Are you always the one giving unconditionally but not receiving unconditionally? If you have answered yes to any of these questions, it is time to realize that you are in a toxic relationship that is undoubtedly poisoning you and slowly destroying your emotional, physical, and mental health.

Examples of Toxic Relationships

Here are some examples of toxic relationships:

- Parents who are hypercritical of their daughters to the point where the daughter's sense of self and personal confidence and esteem are destroyed.

- Men whose childhood fights escalate into adult attacks of sarcasm, power struggles, unfounded accusations, and domestic violence and abuse.

- Women who compete with each other to the point of sleeping with another woman's husband.

- Parents who are so concerned with keeping up with the Joneses that they ignore their children's needs.

- Parents who only show interest in their children if the children do everything the parents want them to into adulthood.

Have you ever given these excuses for toxic relationships? "Well, my friend only gets on my nerves sometimes, but she is an only child so she is used to having her way." "My boyfriend is having a hard time finding a job so he needs me to be encouraging. I cannot expect that from him right now because he has so much on his mind." "Since my father died, my mother cannot focus on anything. I have to be there for her all the time. She needs me all the time." "Oh, my father-in-law is not the type of person to say thank you. He's an old Navy man." "My husband had a rough childhood and his parents never showed him affection." "My sister (or mother) had a lot on her plate when she raised us by herself, and now she just shows a lot of tough love to make sure we were the best we can be." Does any of this sound familiar? I am sure you can think of your own testimony of why someone acts toxically, and is unable to give back to you in the same way you provide to them emotionally, spiritually, physically, or mentally. You may be in a toxic relationship and be totally unaware. A toxic relationship can make you question your own judgment.

With whom do you think you may have a toxic relationship? Why?

_____
_____
_____

What Are These People Like?

Dominating and manipulative people are everywhere, and I am sure you know one or two. They insist on doing and having everything their way. They may seem charming or friendly, but their goal is to have their way in the end. Many of these people (the "toxins") have low self-confidence and self-esteem, and are unaware of their shortcomings. They may be manipulative to maintain a sense of control and power. Most of their victims have less knowledge, confidence, esteem, and power than they do. If the toxic person believes that they are losing control, they may become more aggressive to assure their control over you.

Normally, the "toxins" can actually see the greatness in their victim, but will resort to unhealthy, controlling behaviors to diminish the strengths of their victim. The victim may lean on the toxic person as their self-esteem and confidence begins to plummet. They do not realize that they are being sucked into a very, very unhealthy relationship, which is based on control and manipulation.

Noticing the Toxic Signs

Toxins start slowly and work their way up to take over. They creep in and wear down your resistance. Suddenly, you may realize that you are really in an unhealthy relationship and wonder how in the world do you get out.

Maybe the relationship started out smoothly, but one day a BIG flag went up as a warning that something was very, very wrong. When did the signs begin to present themselves that this was an unhealthy and toxic person? Did you feel like you wanted to run away and escape? Did this person tend to take charge and want total control of you and your behavior?

The 'take charge' attitude might be flattering in the beginning, and you may admire that character trait. During this stage, the 'orders' and domination may be in the form of a soft question or suggestion, "Hey, would you mind…?" and you think nothing of it. Soon after, the suggestion turns into an assumption, "I really know that you're going to……. ." Not soon after that, it is a demand or order, "You had better do this." Some toxic persons may resort to verbal, emotional, or physical abuse if you do not comply. They may also resort to manipulation or humiliation.

If you are not in an equal and balanced relationship, are being forced to do things you would not normally do, or are put in a bind as you struggle to meet the other persons needs, you are in a toxic relationship. This toxic person may not be able to be reasoned with about changing their ways because you are so uncomfortable. If this makes you uncomfortable or scared after the first or second try (and with constant resistance), the only thing you can do is to RUN! Sooner rather than later is best.

What are some of the toxic signs that you have you noticed in your relationships?

_____
_____
_____
_____

How Do I Know?

Figuring out how you know is easy. Deciding that you want to do something about this relationship is more difficult. Ask yourself these questions:

1. Does the person with whom you are in a relationship want everything their way, or want to constantly convince you that their way is the right way and your way is wrong or weak?____

2. Do you find yourself agreeing with the person often, even if you are not sure if it is right, legal, or consistent with your values/morals?____

3. Does the relationship make you feel stronger, encouraged and loved, or weaker, discouraged, and unloved?____

If you answered "yes" to questions 1 and 2 and agreed to the latter in question 3, you now know you are in a toxic relationship. The longer the relationship has existed and the more frequent interaction you have, the harder it is to walk away or distance yourself from this person. You may need professional help with a therapist, counselor, or clergy to deal with and improve your confidence and self-esteem. Whatever you do, don't remain in a toxic the relationship. Seek help from a friend, family member, clergy, or professional counselor or therapist to help guide you and gain the strength to walk away.

How Did it Happen?

Begin to consider all the people in your life who may exhibit unhealthy behaviors. List people in your personal life who:
Are **Insensitive** and critical:
Are **Irresponsible** and do not admit their errors or faults:
Are **Envious** and jealous:
Have **Personality** clashes with you:
Attempt to **Control** you:
Try to **Limit Your Growth:**

Are **Demeaning:**

Are **Dishonest:**

How have these people made you feel? (i.e. angry, resentful, etc). Place words in the following boxes that describe what affect these toxic people have had in your life. (disruptive, insecurity, brokenness, etc.)

Can Toxic Relationships be Made Healthy?

Toxic relationships can be corrected if the toxic person values the relationship enough to be ready to take the necessary steps to truly listen to the problems and consider the consequences of their past behavior. They must be open to understanding your perspective and feelings. They must begin to look at you without judgment or need to criticize, and correct their behaviors, which will result in a healthier relationship with you.

What If I Am In a Toxic Relationship? What Do I Do Now?

You may or may not want to hear this, but if you are in a toxic relationship, you may be playing a pivotal role in **"feeding" or enabling the toxic behavior,** thus giving it more power. There is the good chance that the toxic person will not change. You do not have to maintain "unconditional love" if you are being emotionally, physically, or mentally abused. If the toxic person does not change, you must protect yourself and move on with your life *without this person.* (If this person is a family member, you may wish to discuss with them *why* you are distancing from them emotionally. Let them know you simply will not tolerate the toxic behavior any longer.) Love yourself enough to know when to walk away from the toxic person who is poisoning your life.

When the relationship ends, you may find yourself resentful and bitter that you stayed in a toxic relationship too long, thus lowering self-esteem and self-worth. It is time to rebuild your life with healthy "safe" people whom love and support you. The way others treat you is a direct reflection as to how you feel about yourself. Begin to love yourself, and embrace your strengths and value as a human. You must fully love yourself before you can allow anyone else to be a part of your inner circle—that close place to your heart that very few are allowed to enter. Do not be afraid to be alone as you learn to become your own best friend. Become comfortable with yourself. You will begin to attract more positive people, because we tend to attract people similar to ourselves. The healthier you are, the better the chances of you opening yourself up to new, exciting healthy relationships! Once you strengthen yourself, the right people will be attracted to you, and that inner voice will direct you to the proper people, places, and situations that will edify, fortify, and help you become the person you desire and need to be. If you begin to "settle" for someone who is poisonous because you don't wish to be alone, then the cycle has begun again! Don't settle for a toxic person. You don't deserve it! You deserve the best!

Re-Building Your Life!

If you are currently in a toxic relationship, say this out loud, **"Enough is enough! I'm walking away!"** I did not hear you; say it one more time. **"Enough is enough! I'm walking away!"** Great! Now it is time to work on you.

Tips For Rebuilding Your Life.

1. Rebuild confidence, self-esteem, and self-worth by talking kindly to yourself.

2. Surround yourself with truly supportive people who love and care about you, encourage your progress, and enjoy your company without trying to change you or make you feel inferior, insignificant, or stupid.

3. Enhance your listening skills to detect toxic people that may come into your life. Be very aware of early signs that lead to controlling behaviors.

4. Connect with your inner voice, your intuition, on whether to move forward with a new relationship. Trust your instincts.

Ways to "De-Tox" Yourself

- Spend time alone doing what you love.
- Plan a fun get-away with a special friend or by yourself.
- Look into a mirror and say, "I love me!"
- Create a new life for yourself with loving, positive people.
- Forgive yourself.
- Forgive the toxic person.
- Commit to never, ever entering into a toxic relationship again.

Enjoy your new freedom! You are a person deserving of all that is good in life. If you are in a toxic relationship, end it. Commit yourself to living the rest of your life knowing that you can create the life you want, and you do not ever have to settle again. With that, I close with a personal gift for you.

Personal Affirmation

"I love me and I know my worth. I respect myself and others will have to do the same or there will be no room for them in my life. I will not waste my time and energy on toxic people. Life is too short, time is too precious, and I love me too much."

ABOUT THE AUTHOR

ROSEMARY MEDEL

A City Planner for the last seventeen years in Southern California, Rosemary has worked for the cities of Huntington Beach, Cypress and Signal Hill. A Bachelor of Fine Arts degree with an emphasis in Environmental Design, California State University at Fullerton has prepared Ms. Medel for her current profession in Land Use Planning. She feels strongly about giving back to her community and has volunteered her Planning expertise to the community where she currently resides. Rosemary is a former Planning Commissioner for the City of La Habra where she assisted in guiding development during her three-year term. Currently, Rosemary is a Realtor, and is the owner and president of The Medel Group. Her firm is committed to training and preparing its clients facing risks with confidence, develop their professional image through improved public speaking and presentation skills. She is a co-author of *You're on Stage! Image, Etiquette, Branding & Style, Emotional Wellness for Women: Mind Body & Spirit, Survival Guide for Overcoming Obstacles, Transition & Change, Women as Leaders* and slated to co-author future PWN books titled, *Beyond the Body! Developing Inner Beauty, Young Man's Guide for Personal Success*, and *The Baby Boomer's Handbook for Women*.

Rosemary is a certified trainer in Woman's Issues and a certified Professional Coach and is an International Advisory Board member of the Professional Woman Network. She is also a member of both The Professional Woman Network International Speakers Bureau and the National Association of Female Executives. Rosemary is available for personal and professional coaching sessions.

Her most important role and accomplishment has been raising her two grown children Rosalie and Eli.

Contact
Rosemary Medel
The Medel Group
P.O. Box 2204
La Habra, CA 90632-2204
rosemedel@juno.com
www.TheMedelGroup.com

NINE

THE CHAMELEON: THE ART OF TRANSITION AND CHANGE

By Rosemary Medel

By definition, transition is to change in form or appearance. Transition is also to change in condition, nature or character. Is it not wonderful to think that we can control our lives? We accept that change will happen, but we believe that somehow we affect change by our mere desire. I would theorize that transition is the acceptance of and the preparation for change. Let me give you an example.

At nineteen years of age I received my cosmetology license from the State of California. After working full-time in the trade for four years, I felt I was not living up to my potential. Although working with such fun hairstylists kept me constantly laughing and I enjoyed the creative part of my job, it was not enough. I was told by one hairstylist who was at least fifteen-years older than I that my ambition was due to my youth. With time it would subside, she said. I just wanted to feel that I was truly accomplishing something and impacting the lives of others by more than just providing a great haircut!

There was a desire inside of me to create a better expression of my spirit. I had to develop my mind! I started college at the age of 27, while married and with my three-year old daughter, Rosalie, who was starting pre-school. I was overwhelmed, but I had an opportunity to learn whatever I desired. Taking my education one year at a time, it took me eleven consecutive years to obtain my bachelors degree. What was surprising to me is that I thought I was finished with my education once I graduated. I was a city planner, which would seem to be a good career move, right? To my surprise, this was just the beginning of my education! You see, once the mind is open to all that is possible, your spirit will soar. Our interests change and evolve. One thought leads to more learning and more desire to experience what the world has to offer, and one dream leads to another. Today, as an entrepreneur owning several businesses, my true calling is revealing itself to me, which is to impact the lives of other by helping them find their life path.

How could I have imagined, as a kid from East Los Angeles California, that thirty years later I would be sharing my life stories with my readers? So what really changed in me? What changed was my **Perception** of myself!

Perception: The Struggle Within

You must take small steps at first to gather your thoughts and create a plan for your life journey. You want to map out what is it you want to accomplish, yet remain open-minded enough to be able to change directions when the opportunity arises. If you want to change in the area of your career, you must seek out mentors and develop self-motivation. So, now you start building your **Team** for success! Your team members can be any of the following:

- **Husband:** If you are married and your husband has experience in management, supervision, college courses, or a vocational trade, he is a great resource for you!

- **Siblings:** If you have a brother or sister that has transitioned more in their career or in life, learn from them, too.

- **Friends:** Start a list of those you know. Share with a friend that you trust enough for them to be a part of your dream. Seek a friend that will not criticize, but support what you want to accomplish. They will become a great resource for you, and mentor you, as well.

- **Books:** Seek out the subject matter you are interested in and read, study, absorb everything on the subject. Within these books even more information will be provided, such as resources to learn more on the subject matter. Read inspiration books, as well. They will provide the motivation you will need to stay on course.

- **Supervisors:** Every great supervisor knows that when an employee feels that they are contributing to the betterment of the organization, they do a better job because they take ownership for the success of the company. Share your desire to advance with your supervisor so that they are on board with your goals.

- **On the Job Work Training:** Jobs pay for their employees to increase their skills and knowledge as an incentive to retain talent. Take advantage of this benefit. They also offer tuition reimbursement programs in which you pursue a degree and they reimburse your costs for tuition (and sometimes book costs).

- **Small Business Association (SBA):** The SBA is a wonderful organization to help launch new businesses. They provide loan assistance, training, and mentoring for new business owners. They have the SCORE program, which is a mentoring program for new business owners being mentored by retired executives! There are loan programs for women and minority owned businesses as well.

When we are creating a plan to get to the next level in your professional or personal growth, your team is **CRITICAL**!

Empowerment Skills

So, how does one continue to grow? Keep reinventing yourself. Look at those who continue to re-invent themselves. How about Al Gore? He was the Vice President of the United States, and has recently won the Nobel Peace Prize for his work to prevent Global Warming! Talk about changing direction.

Now let us focus on **you**!

1. In the past five years, how have you changed?

_____
_____
_____

2. Did you change your perception of yourself?
_____
_____
_____

3. Did others change their perception of you?
_____
_____
_____

The path to change is not always an easy one. As a hairstylist, I received criticism because I wanted to attend college. I was called the "college-student," as I walked into the salon. (Perhaps this was passive-aggressive behavior toward me. I felt that I was being teased because I wanted to continue my education.)

You must stay focused on the goal and not letting anyone or anything change your course. You will be constantly tested as to the commitment of your journey. Do you have what it takes to achieve your dreams? I would venture to say yes, or you would not be reading this book!

Moving Forward

You need to become the leader of your life! Make no excuses and have no regrets. Yes, this means go for it! A dear friend by the name of Barbara Holderness (a former hairstyling client who became one of my mentors and a dear friend) gave me a porcelain box as a holiday gift one year, which read, **"Never Complain, Never Explain."** Twenty-five years later I still have this box. Barbara has passed on, but I continue to live by that saying. To me, the saying means do not complain about the life you have chosen, and do not feel the need to justify your reasons for your life's journey. I take full responsibility for my life and make no excuses!

If your intention is to live a life of integrity, make no excuses for obstacles that have been in your way. The "**Blame Game**" is over!

Who or What Has Held You Back?
- Not having been born into wealth
- Not starting college young
- Not marrying well
- Having a child too young
- Having too many children
- Having married too young
- Having married too old
- Being a woman
- Being a minority
- Being too thin or fat
- Being too short or too tall
- A Glass Ceiling I have to break through
- Too old to move up in my company

Are you tired of this list yet? Don't you want to yell **ENOUGH?!** Who or what have you blamed in the past for your life's problems and having difficulty in certain areas?

1. _____
   _____
   _____
   _____
   _____

2. _____
   _____
   _____
   _____
   _____

3. _____
   _____
   _____
   _____
   _____

4. _____
   _____
   _____
   _____
   _____

5. _____
   _____
   _____
   _____

Facing Change With Confidence

To overcome the "Blame Game", it is important to understand and reflect on what you have accomplished in life, in spite of challenges. List below what you have achieved and what the obstacles were:

Achievement	Obstacle

List all the ways you have transitioned in life (i.e. college, marriage, children, new career, loss of job, divorce, empty nest, etc.) and your feelings before and after the transition (i.e. fear, apprehension, joy, etc.)

Transition	Feelings Before	Feelings After

Facing Your Fear!

There is nothing to fear about transition and change, other than fear itself. You have had many successful changes in your life and will have many in the future. But, it is best to prepare and research for future changes. Consider the following:

Exercise

1. What changes do you anticipate in your life during the next year?
- _____
- _____
- _____

2. What changes do you anticipate during the rest of your life? How will you prepare for these changes?
- _____
- _____
- _____
- _____
- _____

Embracing the Unknown.

Once you have charted your goals, future changes, and anticipated transitions, let go and trust that your have prepared for the unforeseen. Don't fill yourself with anxiety. Move forward with your goal. Know that the goal you set is attainable, yet difficult. Know that your goal may change in route, but stay adaptable. Remember the chameleon. This unique little animal adapts constantly to its environment. Don't let minor obstacles derail your dreams. Dream big! Have the optimism of a child and the wisdom of an experienced adult. Develop an attitude of understanding that everything is possible.

Afraid to Change

Change requires an assessment of your current situation. Can things get better? Can you learn to adapt to a new situation? You must believe in your ability to change your life. BELIEVE and it shall be so. Remember the times you have changed in the past. Whether your new change is involving the end of a poisonous relationship, relocating, finding a new job, or deciding to start your own business, believe that you can make it happen, and that you will find a way to succeed. Face your fear, but do it anyway!

Life is always about change. As a woman, you have faced transition from the day you were born. You were a new baby, entered school, made new friends, and may have entered college, married, lost your parents and grandparents, divorced, had health challenges, and dropped out of relationships that were poisonous to your physical, emotional, or spiritual health. But you made it.

You are here today and challenging yourself once again to meet new changes and transitions with grace, dignity, and an abundance of strength. May you have the courage to always remind yourself of the successes you have had in life during past obstacles when changes occurred. You have the strength to do it again and again.

Notes:

ABOUT THE AUTHOR

Violet Mathis

Violet Mathis is President and CEO of The V Factor. She specializes in international workshops, seminars and coaching for self empowerment. Her background is in dentistry and has been a Registered Dental Hygienist for thirty years. Opening her own management consulting company in 2000, Violet is a certified consultant for Bent Erickson & Associates, employment law and human resource specialist, as well as IPM (Integrated Performance Management). She is also a member o SCN (Speakers & Consultants Network), as well as ADMC (Academy of Dental Management Consultants). She is a member of NAFE (National Association of Female Executives) and was the Governor of Who's Who International.

Violet has lived overseas and is an international author and speaker. She is a Certified Diversity Trainer, A Certified Life Coach, and a Certified Wellness Trainer. She has worked in the healthcare field, interior design, sales, and is forever volunteering for various social and charitable organizations.

Violet Mathis has a passion for people. She always sees the best in each person and has the ability to bring out their best qualities. She loves to travel and is always eager for more knowledge. Having a positive attitude is of the utmost importance in her life.

Violet is also co-author of "Women's Survival Guide For Overcoming Obstacles, Transition, and Change".

Contact:
Violet L. Mathis
(678) 644-9499
vlmathis@bellsouth.net
www.protrain.net
www.pwnbooks.com

TEN

VICTIM VS. SURVIVOR

By Violet Mathis

Have you ever had anything happen to you and wonder, "Why Me?" Was your first, instant thought about being a "victim"? Usually the first reaction for most of us is that we have been singled out for this event, and the thought process is almost always negative. Once we encounter obstacles in our lives, we take on an attitude about the event. But attitude becomes the most important element to becoming a "survivor". Each day we have a choice about our attitude and how our day will actually go. If we have a positive attitude, we generally always have a good day. First, we must acknowledge it, see it, and then we believe it. Anne Frank said, "Then, without realizing it, you try to improve yourself at the start of each new day; of course you achieve quite a lot in the course of time. Anyone can do this; it costs nothing and is certainly very helpful. Whoever doesn't know this must learn and find by experience that a quiet conscience makes one strong." Upon doing this, your true "Inner Beauty" will evolve, and you will shine.

First, let us define exactly what the difference is between the two terms. According to the Merriam-Webster Dictionary, a "**victim**" is someone that is injured, destroyed, or sacrificed under any of various conditions, or one that is subjected to oppression, hardship, or mistreatment. This could be a victim of the social system, or a victim of cancer, automobile accident, murder, abuse, or even a victim of political attacks. "**Survivor**", on the other hand, is one who survives or outlives another person, or any time, event, or thing. As you can see, victim can encompass many different venues; however, becoming a survivor may take different roads along the way to recovery.

In the victim mentality, everyone else gets blamed for whatever is going on. The victim believes that the future only holds bad things for them. Once out of an abusive situation, they wonder how and when it stops playing a part in their lives. The BIG difference now is that the physical or emotional abuse is no longer happening in their world. However, the excess baggage that is carried wears them down and keeps them from moving forward. The process follows a pattern:

- Anger
- Resentment
- Blame Game
- Victim Mentality

There seems to be an expectation that things will go wrong because "bad things always happen to me". The victim surrenders the power of their life, and feels that the world owes them and is disappointed and angry when the world doesn't deliver.

What about those who were abused as children? Unfortunately, some of them never are able to move out of the "victim" mode. Abused spouses become victims and find it difficult to move forward. For those who are fortunate enough to want to become "survivors", there actually is a process to getting there. Forgiveness must come into play by forgiving yourself as well as forgiving others. This does not mean you forget, but holding on to the bitterness only empowers the other person, and prohibits you from healing totally.

Four years ago in April, I went in for a routine ob-gyn checkup, only to be sent off for the dreaded mammogram. There was the retake of the mammogram, the biopsy, and the final call saying that I had been diagnosed with breast cancer. All of this sounds quite cut and dried, but it definitely was anything but that. It is amazing how different people react to such information. At first I was numb, in disbelief, devastated, and then probably hysterical. I seem to remember crying forever, and then I remember calling a friend; or maybe they called me (can't remember). We just talked about nothing for most of the evening; certainly nothing concerning my diagnosis.

By the next morning, I was resolved and started doing research and gathering the facts in order to make an informed decision. Once I had talked with my entire group of specialists (there tend to be many at that stage), a decision was made as to how to proceed with treatment. "When" was now the issue. I was awaiting my first grandchild, and I was determined to see her before going under the knife. My surgeons were not happy with my decision, since I would be postponing my surgery for a couple of months. And as most of us know, time is of the essence during cancer treatment. I, on the other hand, was determined, and so we came to an agreement. Riley Elizabeth Mathis was born in June and I had my surgery one week later. I was able to go into surgery with no regrets. It was important for me to be able to hold her, just in case something went awry. Then, she somehow would know that she had a "GrandV" who loved her, held her, and perhaps touched her life. We all must take responsibility for our life and our actions, and then we truly become survivors.

Upon going to make all the arrangements with my specialists, I was amazed at how they were always talking about how positive my attitude was. My reconstruction surgeon almost fainted when I went to see her. She told me that she would have guessed that I was coming to see her about a little liposuction or some other cosmetic procedure instead of breast cancer. I laughed and said maybe we could talk about this at a later date. All along, I felt very blessed to have the wonderful specialists taking care of me.

One of my best friends, Sarah, was diagnosed with an inoperable brain tumor shortly after my event. She was the epitome of health. She ate properly, ran practically every day, did not smoke, and by most standards should have been the picture of perfect health. But her world as she knew it no longer existed. Everything changed, from being totally independent to not being able to drive herself, work, or run without someone by her side, just in case she went into a seizure. **She did not have a choice as to whether she had the brain tumor, but she did have the choice as to how she handled the situation.** Sarah is my hero because she continues to live a "normal" life, whatever that truly means. She took charge of her own health, and continues to live life and does it well. She is now able to do most of her normal activities on her own. She had a choice as to just give up or decide that life was not so bad. Looking at the glass as half full is by far the better of the two scenarios. Her attitude is amazing, and her inner strength and beauty just makes her glow.

These are just two of the stories, however shortened, that I could relate to. I am sure that in your life you know some incredible people who have gone through adversity and come out as a survivor. Here are a few more names that are well-know to most of us:

- Helen Keller – Blindness
- Lance Armstrong – Testicular Cancer
- Viktor Frankl – Holocaust Survivor
- Tina Turner – Battered by Spouse

It is always a challenge to move from "victim" to "survivor". There is a process:

1. Acknowledge the event.
2. You must suffer and grieve.
3. Believer in self.
4. Challenge the odds.
5. Acknowledge the event.
6. Forgive yourself.
7. Forgive the perpetrator or event.
8. Delete the negative.
9. Decide to move forward.

In the United States, about 51% of women will experience at least one traumatic event in their lifetime, ranging from domestic violence, automobile accident, natural disasters, terrorism, or medical issues. When you have no control, adapt as much flexibility as possible. Winston Churchill once said, "Move quickly through a crisis." That is definitely good advise at any age or level in life. Lingering in the moment, however long, is counterproductive to happiness, and the difference between just existing and actually living.

Changing your attitude is vital to recovery. There is a definite link between attitude and healing. It is not always rational, but it still exists. Change the way you think and watch the transformation People who understand that attitude is vital to recovery will evolve much more quickly. How one views a situation influences emotional and physical reaction. Although a catastrophe is often a shocking experience, it is imperative to put it into perspective. Helen Keller stated, "When one door of happiness closes, another opens; but often we look so long at the closed door that we do not see the one that has been open for us."

One of the best things to remember is that who you are is not defined by the event that happened to you, but what you choose to become. If you sit around and wallow in self-pity, things will not improve. You need to make a conscious decision to move forward and choose who you will become in the future. Many of the wonderful women I have met over the past years are phenomenal. Many of them have overcome adversities of great magnitude, and chose to move forward and become authors, writers, speakers, etc. The fact of the matter is that instead of choosing to stay stagnant and dwell on what had happened to them, they took the positive approach and made things happen for the betterment in their lives. The book "*The Secret*", which was released recently, teaches us to first think it, then to see it, next to believe it, and finally to feel it. It is like having a plan or goal. Writing it down makes it real. We thought it, saw it in writing, believed it would happen or come to us, and finally we could actually feel it happening to us. What a great experience. Remember, it is not always easy to be positive, but if you do not try, you will definitely never get there. The trials in life are just temporary setbacks. It has been said that "Life is 10% of what happens to us and 90% of how we react to it."

Some of the steps in getting where you want to be in life depend on positive influences. A few of these should be added to your life on a daily basis:

- **Humor** – being able to laugh at oneself is so important. Remember, it is ok to make mistakes. That is how we learn. None of us is perfect, and humor can build confidence.
- **Support Systems** – having friends, family, and support groups can get you through the tough times. Let them know what you are doing and why. They will understand and help pull you at your lowest point. Being loved is a powerful healing tool. Don't forget to ask for what you need. Others do not read your mind.
- **Spiritual** – prayer, meditation, or the power of positive thinking lightens the load. You are able to draw from others. When your strength is down, something higher will hold you up.
- **Diet** – nutrition for the body is the healing foundation for growth, whether it is mental or physical.
- **Exercise** – daily activity not only opens your body for healing, but also fuels the brain, which in turn allows you to heal from within. Going back to the basics with just stretching is the perfect start.
- **Hope** – remember, there is always hope when you believe it. Forget the "poor little me mentality". No negative talk. A renewed spirit each day gives us hope for a new beginning.

- **Compassion** – take time out to get out of yourself. There are others who are going through adversities. When you focus on others needs, it is easier to stop dwelling on your situation. Caring for others is a miraculous healer.

We often hear that bad things happen to good people, but guess what? Sometimes good things happen to good people. Make a conscious decision to start a new lease on life. Believe me, what a difference a day makes! Most of the time, we are thinking about what we did in the past and worrying that we should have done something differently, or thinking about what we are going to do later that day or tomorrow. We should learn to live in the moment - live in the now. That time will never be there again. We cannot change what happened in the past, nor do we have control over much of the future. Take time to relax, rest, recuperate, and enjoy loving care. Nothing makes you realize how important living your life each day is until you are diagnosed with cancer or some other major event brings you to your knees. Guess what? None of us is guaranteed the next day so:

- It is imperative to live each day as if it were your last.

- Do not put off until tomorrow what you should do today.

- Make sure you say I love you more often.

- If you see someone who deserves a compliment, do not hesitate to give it. That small act, whether you know the person or not, may be the nicest thing that is said to them all day. It is amazing what a little boost to one's esteem can do to make another's day special.

Remember when you were a child, before society placed its views and values on us, and the sheer pressure of everyday life affected your thinking? We lived a magical world. We believed that people told the truth. We just accepted that laughing was ok (giggling especially was especially fun), jumping up and down with childlike enthusiasm, running to places instead of walking (just because), jumping up and down on the bed with glee, or just being still and watching the grass grow. Somewhere along the way we forgot how simple and fun life was supposed to be.

The next time you are feeling like the "victim", remember to stop, take a deep breath, relax the shoulders, close your eyes, and remember how special you are and how priceless the day is. The life of a "survivor" is waiting for you. All the happiness, health, love, prosperity, and abundance in life are waiting on you. You have the ability to spread the "survivor" mode and mentality around. Attitudes are contagious, whether they are good or bad. Pay attention to the people you are around, as well. You may have to rethink your relationships if individuals have negative personalities. I have had to stop being friends because of negative attitudes. Most of us are very susceptible to what is happening around us. If you are working on maintaining your positive attitude, then you cannot be subjected to negative input and ideas on a continual basis.

Challenge yourself to move from "victim" mentality to "survivor". Control and power are in your hands. It is truly a "survivor's" world, and it can be exciting, fun and challenging. Accept responsibility for your life and you will reap all the joys that you deserve. Learn to truly, deeply appreciate every kindness, laughter, and each day. Maya Angelou once said, "I may be changed by what happens to me, but I refuse to be reduced by it."

Recommend Reading and Resources

The National Center for Victims of Crime, www.ncvc.org

National Organization for Victim Assistance, www.trynova.org

The Secret by Rhonda Byrne

Notes:

ABOUT THE AUTHOR

KAREN BRUNDAGE-JOHNSON

Karen Brundage-Johnson is Founder of Your Image Matters, a consulting and training organization. As a business leader and certified training facilitator, Karen has overseen the training and development of thousands of employees in the telecommunications and hospitality industries. She has been instrumental in implementing programs in personal and professional development, self esteem, career development, women's issues, stress management and diversity. Karen's focus has been on helping individuals assess their behavior to improve interpersonal relationships while gaining a greater appreciation and respect of others and valuing differences.

Karen's credentials include a Post Masters Certificate in Human Resources Management, a Master of Science degree in Business Management/Human Resources Management and a Bachelor of Arts in Psychology.

Karen is also a member of the National Association of Female Executives, the Society for Human Resources Management, New Jersey Organization Development Learning Community, American Association of University Women and Delta Sigma Theta Sorority, Inc., an international public service organization. Karen has been featured in Today's Insurance Professional Magazine; a publication of the National Association of Insurance Women (International).

Contact:
Your Image Matters
PO Box 982
Mays Landing, NJ 08330
(609) 641-5410
yourimagematters@comcast.net

ELEVEN

15 STRATEGIES FOR OVERCOMING NEGATIVE THINKING

By Karen Brundage-Johnson

If you're like most people, you occasionally will talk to yourself. You may say words that others can hear, but most of us, when we talk to ourselves, say the words in our minds.

Your thoughts have a powerful effect on you. They affect your attitude, your physiology, and your motivation to act. Your negative thoughts actually control your behavior. They can make you stutter, drop things, forget your next thought, or breathe shallowly. According to Emmanuel Sequi, research indicates that the average person says about 55,000 words per day to himself or herself; 77% is negative talk.

Negative self-talk such as "That was stupid," "You're a failure," "You can't do that," "They don't like me," "I'm not a speaker," "I'll never lose this weight," "I can't ever seem to get organized," "I'm always late." --- can leave a lasting hurt that usually isn't easy to repair.

Remember from childhood the schoolyard rhyme, "Sticks and stones may break my bones, but names will never hurt me?" Sadly, the negative words and phrases that we hear from ourselves can hurt us and lower our self-esteem. Motivational speaker Les Brown compares negative self-talk to a nail being pounded into a board. Sure, the nail can be removed, but the hole remains until it is filled in and repaired. Words or statements you use to describe yourself (or what is happening to you and how you feel about a situation) can trigger feelings of happiness, unhappiness, or depression. By learning to control your inner conversation or self- talk, you can begin to manage and control your life. Each day of our lives we are faced with challenges or problems to solve. Change is constant and unavoidable, but our ability to succeed comes from how we *deal* with change. Having a positive attitude is critical for success and happiness. It is the key to success in business, and important to building lasting relationships.

When a problem or difficult situation comes up, you must learn to change your language from negative to positive. Try to use the word ***situation*** instead of ***problem***. A problem is something you struggle with and represents a potential loss. A situation is something that you deal with and does not insinuate that it will be a negative outcome. The way you **interpret** the event is what really counts. Perception is reality, and if you face the event perceiving it to simply be a situation that can be handled, you are on your way to a positive outcome.

In her book *Bits and Pieces of My Soul***:** *Remembering What We Already Know*, Carolyn Dixon, M.D. writes that all things in life begin with you. Therefore, it's important to know who you are, what you are, and that for which you stand. Getting to know yourself means making a thorough analysis that begins by finding answers to questions such as, "Who am I?", "What is my purpose?", "What do I value?", "What do I want in life?" or "What are my strengths and weaknesses?"

Exercise: Making it Happen
From deep within ourselves, we get messages. Sometimes the messages say that we are "good" and "doing fine". Sometimes the messages are that we are "stupid", or that "you can't do this."

Write down examples of negative and positive self-talk for the situations below. Describe your feelings. The first has been done as an example. You can also add some other situations to the list.

Situation	Negative Self-Talk	Positive Self-Talk
Example: *Giving a presentation* **Feelings:**	*I'm dull. They won't want to hear from me.* **Frightened**	*I'm interesting. Maybe I'll make a great impression.* **Excited**
1. Have a project deadline **Feelings:**		
2. Need to make a recommendation **Feelings**		
3. Giving an opinion **Feelings**		

Situation	Negative Self-Talk	Positive Self-Talk
4. Making a speech **Feelings**		
5. **Feelings**		
6. **Feelings**		

The 15 Strategies

1. Start by following this basic rule: Talk positively to yourself and to others. What you say to yourself has a profound impact on your self-image, your self-esteem, and your performance as well as eventual success. Remember that your subconscious triggers physiological responses to match the pictures and thoughts that you have of yourself.

2. Make positive communications a habit. Focus on the positive in your self-talk, and all communications. Notice how in these phrases the positive words express confidence, commitment, and enthusiasm. For example, instead of "I will try", substitute the phrase, "I will." Instead of saying, "I should", insert the phrase, "I will."

3. Use affirmations to enhance your self-esteem. Affirmative statements are positive self-talk statements or reminders to help you communicate effectively. Write down your own affirmations on the back of your business card or small index card. Write a statement such as, "I love and accept myself everyday" or "I am a valuable, lovable person and deserve the best in life." Carry the card with you and practice saying the affirmation several times during the day, especially at night before going to bed and after awakening in the morning. Whenever you say the affirmation, allow yourself to experience positive feelings about yourself.

Exercise: Nothing Ventured, Nothing Gained

A. Some people **don't try** new things because they're scared. List the best and the worst that could happen if you……….

	Best	Worst
Wrote a novel		
Tried a new hairstyle		
Introduced yourself to someone new		
Learned a foreign language		

B. List some additional activities **you could** try, and give the worst and best things that could happen.

I could try:	The worst that could happen	The best that could happen

C. Write 3 examples of negative self-talk that you might use to talk yourself out of trying something new.

1. _____
2. _____
3. _____

D. Write 3 positive self-talk examples of what you could say to yourself to provide courage.

1. _____
2. _____
3. _____

4. Change Negative Self-Talk into Positive Self-Talk: Negative self-talk statements like, "I can't handle this!" or "This is too difficult!" are damaging because they increase stress in a situation and they stop you from searching for solutions. Try turning these statements into questions such as, "How can I handle this?" or "How is this difficult?" They are more hopeful, and open up your imagination to new possibilities.

5. Get to Know Yourself. Don't be afraid to understand yourself. Learn who you really are inside of your fears, fantasies and desires. Write down a thought or two at the end of each day that describes who you are. Knowing yourself will help you overcome barriers that stand in the way of happiness and success. As adults, we can choose the messages we accept or reject. As Eleanor Roosevelt said, "No one can make you feel inferior without your permission." "Building high self-esteem is a process, not something you can develop overnight," says Jeffrey Keller. Yet, I believe every person has the capacity of high self-esteem. The question is, are you ready to make a commitment to increase your self-esteem? If your answer is yes, here are 12 more strategies to get you started:

6. Keep a Journal: Carry a journal around with you and jot down negative comments when you think them; write a general summary of your thoughts at the end of the day.

7. Stop Comparing Yourself to Other People. There will always be someone who has more of whatever you want, and others who have less. If you play the comparison game, you'll run into too many "opponents" who you can't defeat.

8. Stop Putting Yourself Down. You can't develop high self-esteem if you repeat negative phrases about yourself and your abilities. Whether speaking about your appearance, career, relationships, financial situation, or any other aspect of your life, avoid self-deprecating comments.

9. Mirror, Mirror On the Wall – Positive Self-Talk Wanted. Every day look at yourself in the mirror and affirm that you are a good person. This technique will help you feel better about yourself and overcome obstacles.

10. Be Responsible for Your Feelings. Feelings and emotions can be quite powerful. Sometimes your feelings seem stronger than you are. But, feelings are made up of two parts—emotions and thoughts. The emotions—like anger, love and fear—may come upon you quickly, but their power depends on what you think about them. You must decide how to act on your feelings. You can either hold onto them, or let them pass. Being responsible for your feelings puts you in charge, and makes you more powerful than they are.

11. Choose to Lift Yourself Up. If you don't like something about yourself, change it. If you can't change it, accept it. But, don't beat yourself up with negative self-talk. You're not likely to change for the better when you say to yourself things like, "*Get out of bed, you lazy bum!*", "*How could you be so stupid?*" or "*When will you ever learn?*" Instead, if you encourage yourself with positive feedback such as, "*It's hard, but you can do it!*", "*Everyone makes mistakes*" or "*You'll do better next time*", you'll feel better about trying to change things you don't like.

12. Give Yourself Positive Rewards. When you do something you're proud of, tell yourself you did well. Give yourself a small reward. If you wait for others to praise you, you may grow resentful if the praise doesn't come. But, if you pat your own back, the good feeling will stay with you longer — if you let it.

13. Forgive Yourself. You wouldn't keep scolding a friend for making a mistake or missing an opportunity, so don't do that to yourself. Forgive yourself for making a mistake. Then, figure out what lesson you can learn, and use it to make better choices next time.

14. Enjoy Your Successes. Most people can remember the details of painful or embarrassing events that happened many years ago. What if you could remember just as well some triumph that made you feel really good about yourself? Keep that memory with you and think about it at least once a week.

15. Accept All Compliments With "Thank You." Have you ever received a compliment and replied, "Oh, it was nothing." When you reject a compliment, the message you give yourself is that you are not worthy of praise. Respond to all compliments with a simple, "thank you."

Exercise: Getting to Yes! Your Inner Voice

Having positive self-talk is all about the language you use. We have two internal voices – the **Yes** and the **No**. The good news for learning and living is that we can program our Inner Voice, and can become the voice and the person we wish to be. What we say with our Inner Voice will show up in our Outer Self as a positive person. Let's practice getting to your YES inner voice:

NO	YES
No, I can't do it!	I've got this task to do: *YES* I'll give it my best shot!
This is silly, this is stupid.	I will be able to do this.
I can't do this: it's too hard.	There is a solution and I'll find it.
I'll do it tomorrow (next week).	I'll do it now!
I'm hopeless. This is impossible. I'm not even going to try!	Sounds good, I'll give it a go.
It's not my fault, so don't blame me (it is their fault … spouse, children, manager, co-worker).	Yes, I made that mistake, and I can learn from the experience.
I don't like that person.	That person has some really good points.
I'm hopeless at …	I'm good at … (writing, teaching).

Medical professionals are taking note of the mind-body relationships in their treatment of patients. Self-talk is a health behavior that has potentially far-reaching effects. The use of positive self-talk has been linked to the reduction of stress. Positive self-talk means purposely giving yourself positive reinforcement, motivation, and recognition the same way you would do for a friend. Congratulate yourself when you do well, and remind yourself of your abilities, accomplishments, strengths and skills. Keep a to-do list, check off accomplishments, and review your progress periodically.

Make self-talk work for you. What you habitually say to yourself has a very profound impact on your self-image, your self-esteem, and your performance, as well as your eventual success.

Reading Resources

Bits and Pieces of My Soul: Remembering What We Already Know by Carolyn Dixon, M.D.

The Use—and Abuse—of Negative Thinking by R.D. Grainger, American Journal of Nursing, (1991).

Building Self-Esteem—How to Transform Your Self-Talk to Build Your Self-Esteem by Emmanuel Segui, *E-zine article,* September 2007.

If Life is a Game, These are the Rules by Cherie Carter-Scott.

Notes:

ABOUT THE AUTHOR

Linda Farr

Linda Farr is founder and sole proprietor of A Spark Within Coaching. As a mid-life transition and business coach, she specializes in empowering others to clarify the truths, beliefs and attitudes that direct their lives, leading to increased self-satisfaction and success both on a personal and a professional level.

Ms. Farr completed two years of training with The Coaches Training Institute, a premier global training school for life coaches and is a member of the International Coach Federation Her expertise is also based on the culmination of a variety of life experiences. After earning her bachelor's degree in Education from Northern Illinois University and teaching in an academic setting for eight years, she followed the entrepreneurial call and opened several floor covering and furniture businesses that flourished for 25 years. During that time, she embraced marriage and motherhood, obtained her private pilot's license, owned and managed several real estate ventures, and took time to enjoy a horse, dogs, oil painting and travel. She also enjoys being a member of The Professional Woman Network.

Ms. Farr shares her experiences and insights with others supporting and guiding them through important life decisions. She specializes in:
- Mid-Life Coaching. This age brings different experiences and decisions. She leads clients in examining and resolving their issues.
- Business Coaching. Her business programs include Illuminating Marketing, Mastermind Brainstorming Sessions, consulting and development.
- Writing. She develops programs and activities for coaches and trainers, and produces workshops for educational and speaking events.

Ms. Farr is available for one-on-one and group coaching, in person and via phone.

Contact
Linda Farr
A Spark Within Coaching
W332 S450 Government Hill
Delafield, WI 53018
(414) 315-2021
sparkcoaching@wi.rr.com
www.asparkwithincoaching.com

TWELVE

CREATING YOUR SPACE FOR PEACE

By Linda Farr

You probably already have a concept of what your "Peaceful Space" might feel like—relaxed, supported, surrendered, confident, and outside of time. Though it presents a different picture to each of us, you will recognize it when you feel yours. The intention of this chapter is to guide you so that you may connect, experience, and live more often in your Peaceful Space.

In this chapter I will share with you:

- Glimpses into the Peaceful Spaces that others have built into their lives.

- A self-assessment to gauge your Peace Quotient.

- Techniques to use in maintaining your Space for Peace.

Defining a Peaceful Life

In preparing this chapter, I questioned many individuals about what living a peaceful life meant to them, and how they succeeded in maintaining it. Their insights were varied (as would be expected), but the richness and creativity of their responses was impressive. Some envision a scene, real or imaginary. Some find peace through their breathing or other physical practice. Others repeat specific words that are personally empowering.

Whatever the technique, a peaceful life brings feelings of safety, inner knowing, loving, appreciation, surrender, empowerment, timelessness, and self-confidence. Compare that to your daily life! For most, this feeling of serenity is anchored by a sense of being part of a spiritual connection to God or a universal power. It is a space that once felt, calls to be revisited. It seems to exist along side of our reality, like a parallel universe. We can slip into it when we relax, pause our thoughts, or meditate. I invite you to experiment and play with the concepts presented. The rewards will dwarf your efforts and last a lifetime.

The following excerpts are descriptions of others' Peaceful Spaces. Read the following excerpts and enjoy them; perhaps one will ignite your imagination and take you for a visit.

1. "Being Peaceful is like riding a wave, running a marathon, or experiencing any exceptional high. I feel connected to an energy source that is endless. Events flow, timing works out magically, and coincidences happen. I have learned (usually) to release thoughts of control and judgment, because what I once labeled as 'bad' often turns around and becomes my biggest blessing. There is a lot of trust involved, but then I relax into Peace and just ride the wave. My mind keeps focusing in the present because that is where I am and the action is taking place." –Carol B.

2. "Here I go – stream of consciousness – I'm getting the image of a still lake. Yes, things can disturb it, but those things are momentary disruptions that just play on the surface. Even if they do kick up mud at the bottom, things settle back into tranquility again. So, it's about having that tranquil state be more your norm, your set point. When I was younger, I don't think that was the case. I was agitated a lot – by perceived unfairness, or by my own demons. They're still there on occasion, but they don't define my experience. It took a long time for me to discover that the still lake was possible, but now that I know, it's a treasured refuge." –JoAnne O'B-L

3. "I have a 'workshop' in my mind that I visit to be peaceful and comfortable, or productive and achieving. I can go anytime I want. It is located in a log cabin situated on a high hill overlooking mountains, a forest, and a large blue lake. As I enter the door, a warm, soothing, yellow light covers every part of me. It removes any negative thoughts, replacing them with positive ones. In front of me stretches a long, dark brown table that contains all the equipment that I need to conduct my work. If I need anything, it instantly appears for me. I sit in a comfortable chair that glides wherever I want. This space has no limitations and holds everything that I need." – John F.

4. "I begin with a ritual for clarity. I light a candle and anoint myself with oil on my forehead, heart and solar plexus while asking my spirit for peace in my thoughts, feelings, and images. I focus on feeling my inner body and allow a deeper sense of relaxation while concentrating on my breath. Soon, I enter a space of deep stillness, and I just rest there for as long as I have time. Time gets distorted, and when I return I am in the energy of Peace. My focus becomes maintaining this energy throughout the day. Through practice, I enter this state more quickly and maintain it for longer periods of time. I

call it my Peace Training. It empowers me in making conscious choices about what will or will not disturb MY Peace." - Cynthia F.

5. "I believe Peace is my connection to Divine Source. When I notice I'm out of peace, I stop and invite peace back into my life... I imagine White Light glowing inside of me and I soften, breathe, and receive... I feel my outer body let go of tension and relax from head to foot... Soon, I realize I'm back in the arms of love, being carried, and feeling that peace that passeth all understanding." – Bonnie K.

6. "When upset, I have a mantra that I repeat to center and calm my thoughts. As I speak it, I relax into the focus of that one thought. My emotions and mind empty; the space is filled with an inner confidence and knowing. The picture forms of a tuning fork ringing deep within my body. The vibrating waves go out, filling the air. The waves radiate out, calming my life. Situations soften and I smile more often. The more I practice, the more effective it becomes for me." – Linda F.

7. "I have realized my Peaceful Life. For me, this means living balanced and centered most of the time, despite the chaos of life. My life is full to the point of overflowing, but instead of feeling stressed, I feel content. I know I have exactly what I need in each moment; I have all the time I need. When I catch myself becoming stressed, I am usually able to switch back into my Peaceful Life. From there, life flows and I am a part of that flow. I have complete trust in my place in the universe and feel totally supported. My gateway to this peace and centeredness is Kundalini Yoga, which I practice daily." – Jamie D.

Now, it is your opportunity to describe your own Peaceful Space. You may borrow from the above or invent your own. It may be a real or imagined place in which you could be safe and secure. There are two aspects to include. One involves describing the actual appearance of the place (as in the workshop). Include the sounds, objects, colors and smells that attract you.

The other aspect consists of the sensations you have when you are there. Picture yourself in it. Allow your imagination to expand. How does Peace feel to you? Record it below, and be comfortable knowing it will evolve over time as your practice and confidence grows.

My Peaceful Space:
_____
_____
_____

Assessing Your Peace Quotient
The following brief assessment will provide feedback on how Peaceful your life is presently. Score each statement from 1 to 5, with 1 being in total agreement and 5 being completely opposed.

	I connect to a satisfying state of Peace each day.
	I accept my life as it is RIGHT NOW. I am content.
	I am able to turn off the chattering voices running through my head whenever I want.
	I believe that Peace comes from the silence within. I can experience it by being centered and detached from my busy activities.
	I feel totally supported by the flow of life.
	My life moves at an acceptable speed.

Scoring:
—Add up the number of points you indicated.
—Score the results as follows:

6 to 9 _____ Send me your Peaceful Space. I'll include it in my next article.

10 to 17 _____ You have created some good habits, but you could release deeper.

18 to 25 _____ Relax and unwind. Take 15 minutes daily to practice being at Peace.

26 to 30 _____ Life can be so much more enjoyable. Stretch and open to some new ideas.

Maintaining Your Peaceful Life Tools

You have described your Peaceful Space, and are committed to experiencing the relief it brings. I congratulate you for your attention to your self-care.

This section offers techniques to keep you motivated as you experiment with your Peaceful Space. There will probably be times when you are feeling less enthused. Remember that in order to make changes in your life, you will need to make changes in your attitudes and actions. I suggest that you experiment using each tool. It may take a few attempts before you feel comfortable practicing the new behaviors. Each one can offer a unique piece in your development. Record your experiences in the spaces provided.

#1. Create a Successful Environment for Your Peaceful Space.

- How often will you set aside time for your Peace? Set a schedule on your planner. Once or twice a day is suggested: 10 times is recommended for faster results. It takes 21 days to form a new habit.

- Where will you practice? It is easier to create a habit if you choose the same place.

  _____

- Do you have any special requirements, such as candles, music, quiet, special pictures, etc.?

  _____

- Set yourself up for success. Tell your family that you are serious, and that you need this time without interruption. The more often you connect with your relaxing Peaceful Space, the more you will experience the benefits—and so will your family.

#2. Remember the Times When You Have Connected to Peace.

Haven't you realized that you have already experienced this connection? Maybe you were watching waves, open flames, a baby, or the night sky, walking in nature, gardening, jogging, or creating artwork. You probably experienced this while listening to music or enjoying complete stillness. So many situations are available to you on a daily basis when time seems to stop, your focus narrows, you feel energized and alert. You seem to be in a different, larger dimension.

Record the circumstances that have already brought you Peace. Include your feelings and sensations. If you need more space for your list, be grateful and record them on another sheet.

_____
_____
_____

#3. Observe the Thoughts That Run Through Your Mind.

Research has shown that the average person has 60,000 thoughts each day. Most are repetitive, meaning they repeat out of habit in the background. To clear those thoughts, picture them streaming out of your head and pretend you are just watching them. Try to feel a disconnect between yourself and the chatter. In that space, connect to your Peace. Record below the statements that frequent your mind.

_____
_____
_____

#4. Replace Your Negative Thoughts.

Sometimes you can feel beaten down by the critical, judging chatter that runs through your mind. A visit to your Peaceful Space slows these voices and helps them disappear like smoke. Add your own new powerful voices in the quiet that remains. Make a list of positive affirmations that you can repeat, write, or shout.

Below are listed several general affirmations that can be adapted for your specific situation. Circle the ones that allow you to feel more empowered.

1. I am replacing my old beliefs and allowing more Peace.

2. Sometimes I make too much of my situation. I have really made good progress.

3. I always feel refreshed when I visit my Peaceful Space.

4. I've complained about my situation enough. I think I'll move on and take a new step.

5. I am creating a wonderful, safe, and quiet Peaceful Space.

6. Things always work out for me. _____ will also work out for me.

7. My life is becoming so easy & enjoyable as I allow new Peaceful thoughts to flow.

8. I love and approve of myself; I am happy to be me.

#5. Trust That Once You Claim a Peaceful Life, Events Will Happen to Bring Peace to You.

Begin each day with an attitude of curiosity and gratitude. This openness will allow you to notice the coincidences or inspired actions that are bringing Peaceful changes to your life. Appreciate these small encounters and more will flow. Keep a journal of these coincidences or record them below. An added benefit is that on days when you feel stressed, you can reread them to raise your spirits.

_____
_____
_____

#6. Get Into Physical Motion.

If your mind is locked up, move your body. If you are holding rigidly to the thoughts in your mind, your body is probably tight, as well. So, move your body, dance, spin, walk, or swim, whatever gets you to an 'out of chair' experience. Yell, "I am moving through this situation", or "I am stepping out of my stuck place." Once your body moves, your mind often follows. Your body/mind connection can be a powerful tool for disconnecting your mind and hearing the quiet. Record several physical activities you can begin when you are getting stuck. Include some you could do at your desk or in small spaces, like tightening and releasing various muscle groups.

_____
_____
_____

#7. Ask a Friend or Life Coach For Help.

Coaches are trained, and familiar with reaching new goals. They listen to your concerns, try to find the truth in your story, and brainstorm new possibilities with you. As we confide in one another, hard as the first words are, the relief can flow. We discover we have been harder on ourselves than others are. Once those fears are spoken, they often lose some of their power. The situation becomes easier to live in. List the names of friends or Life Coaches you will contact for support.

_____
_____
_____

#8. Make Decisions From Your Peaceful Space.

Once you are centered and quiet, listen for your inner voice. It is a quiet voice that brings your biggest answers, but is hard to hear when you are busy or taking action. It may come from God, the universe, or a higher power. Whatever has meaning for you. Ask your question, and then let it go. Be open to receiving a word, a new idea, or intuition in the next few days. You'll know it when you hear it. It will stand out, but you may not understand it. As you become more quiet, the voice becomes clearer.

Take this opportunity to have a conversation with your Inner Voice. Thank it for being there when you listen. Let it know that you will be listening more for its input. Record the intuitions you receive.

_____
_____
_____

9. Share This Chapter With a Group of Friends.

Meet with a small group of friends to brainstorm ideas for creating Peaceful Spaces and practicing these tools together. Hold a monthly check-in coffee or dinner for updating your progress, and establishing your new habits. I met with one such group monthly for over five years. My daughter was an infant, and I was feeling isolated. I contacted three women with whom I had wanted to become better friends. I asked if they would be interested in having a simple dinner at my home and getting to know each other better. We all had felt a need, but couldn't find the time. After the first few dinners, we were sharing deeply, and were committed to our continuing friendship. We always had hugs for each other through childbirths, disease, and celebrations. This group had given our lives a continuity and stability. It certainly was worth all the efforts.

List below the names of some friends or acquaintances that you could invite. My experience is that most people would be flattered to be asked.

_____
_____
_____

#10. Express Your Feelings of Discontent, Grief, or Anger.

Act out these feelings, or give them a monster sound. Grunt, yelp, whine or cry. Storm about like King Kong, or whatever comes to mind. Act out the emotion until you are body-tired. You have just cleared the mental energy that was blocking your inner Peace of Mind. Relax into the hidden quiet that was under all that noise. List several places you would feel safe being loud.

_____
_____
_____

#11. Surrender to the Peace You Desire.

Sometimes, in order to enter a Peaceful Space, it is necessary to admit that you don't have all the answers. Often, this realization is preceded by a time (lasting hours to weeks) in which you are locked in your fears, unable to consider new information. You may have a tightness in your chest, your breath may be shallow, sleep may be fitful as your mind races. In the past, you dug in deeper and changed nothing. Now is the time to admit that you need a new answer. Give up your preconceived ideas about how the world should work. Take a breath and release it into the Peaceful Space you have been practicing. Be quiet, surrender into something bigger than you, and relax into the coming relief.

Record your experience, your insights, and the miracles that occur in the following days.

_____
_____
_____

My hope is that this chapter can serve as a guide or motivator for you. As you allow and trust in the letting go, you will receive many benefits. There are more than I have mentioned now, but you will discover them. Play with the techniques or design your own. There are many paths to this Space. I can't imagine my life without mine. Remember that the more often you visit, the more often it follows you home.

ABOUT THE AUTHOR

Dr. Mary Ann Alexander-Wilford

Dr. Alexander-Wilford is a New Jersey certified school counselor at Coopers Poynt Professional Development Middle School and Biology teacher for the adult evening school in Camden New Jersey. She is the founder and CEO of MAW Consulting Services LLC, an educational and personal development consulting firm.

She is also a supervisor of various "SES" (Supplemental Educational Services) programs (Data Friendly Inc., Education Station) that provide math, reading and test preparation to K-12 students. She has presented various workshops and in-services for teachers on testing and closing the achievement gap. She has been an educator for 33 years and is committed to education of children, adolescents and adults encouraging them to be the best they can be.

Dr. Alexander-Wilford serves on the 2007 Professional Woman Network International Board. She focuses on and is certified in the following areas: Leadership skills, Self esteem, Mentoring for our youth and School attendance.

She is a native of Chester, Pennsylvania and currently resides in Bear, Delaware with her husband, Darryl and daughter Cherish. Dr. Alexander-Wilford has a Bachelor's degree in Biology/Pre-Med. from Cheyney State/University, a Master's degree in School Counseling(k-12) from Wilmington College/ University, and Doctorate of Education from Nova Southeastern University.

Dr. Alexander-Wilford interest includes meeting people dancing, walking, being with family members and living life to its fullest. She is an active member of the National and New Jersey Counselor Association, a member of the National Sorority of Phi Delta Kappa, Inc. and Delta Sigma Theta Sorority Inc. She is a former NFL (Philadelphia Eagles) cheerleader and model. Dr. Alexander-Wilford is available to presents new research works and share her skills and experiences as a consultant/presenter, and trainer through seminars and in-services to both local and national organizations business and educational communities.

Contact
MAW Consulting Services, LLC
223 Cornwell Drive
Bear, Delaware 19701.
Email: maa223@aol.com
www.protrain.net

THIRTEEN

BUILDING SELF-ESTEEM

By Dr. Mary Ann Alexander-Wilford

The term "self-esteem", one of the oldest concepts in psychology (also called self-worth, self-confidence, and self respect) reflects a person's overall self-appraisal of their own worth. Self-esteem can also mean one hates oneself. It involves ones mental perception of ones qualities. Self-esteem can truly be defined as appreciating your own worth and importance, and having the character to be accountable for yourself and to act responsibly toward others.

One of the most basic needs is to have a sense of personal worth. This has two elements: **security** and **significance.** Security means being loved and accepted just for you who are, regardless of what you do. This is called "core" self-esteem, and psychologists refer it to as "global" self-esteem, being loved and accepted.

Significance means having meaning and *"purpose in your life",* and being adequate for what you do is referred to as situational self-esteem. It is knowing that we are good at what we do. Our self-esteem develops and evolves throughout our lives as we build an image of ourselves through our experiences with different people and activities.

Experiences during our childhood play a particularly large role in the shaping of our basic self-esteem. When we were growing up, our successes (and failures) and how we were treated by the members of our immediate family, by our teachers, coaches, religious authorities, and by our peers, all contributed to the creation of our basic self-esteem. The problem is that we develop a series of **false assumptions** of what we think will meet our needs **for security and significance.** We usually learn these assumptions in childhood. If we don't experience unconditional love and acceptance as a child, we will experience pressure to have those needs met elsewhere. And if we aren't given a sense of competency and significance in childhood, we will also experience pressure to meet that need elsewhere.

The proper formation of security in childhood—this "intrinsic value"—can be affected by many things, and abuse at many levels is a growing problem. Living with constant ridicule, contempt and negativity can affect a child's security into adulthood. Perhaps you've overheard a parent criticizing a child. It's not just the words that are used, but also the tone of voice that can deeply affect the child.

When you have high self-esteem, you create energy in your life to make things happen. When you feel good about yourself, it is easier to know you matter, and that what you do does make a difference. Be aware that every negative belief diminishes your ability to value yourself.

Healthy Self-Esteem means feeling good about yourself, and does not mean you are conceited. Rather, you have a positive attitude about yourself and pride in your accomplishments. Low self-esteem comes in a variety of packages. Some try to cover up their low self-esteem with lots of accomplishments and trappings, while others almost flaunt their failures. Low self-esteem manifests itself in diverse ways, and is often illusive to self and others.

Symptoms of Low Self-Esteem

Women are remarkably strong individuals who have the capability to battle with demons and conquer the world. But more often than not, it is their own self-confidence that brings them down. That nagging voice in the back of your head that questions your actions, criticizes you looks, and doubts your self-worth can bring any woman (no matter how successful or powerful) to her knees.

Lack of self-esteem closes you to all of the possibilities in life. You act differently, dress in no particular style, and avoid situations that make you uncomfortable. You also may have felt stressed when confronted with new situations, as any type of change may be painful. Lack of self-esteem may drive you to think only of others, and put *your* hopes and dreams on the back burner because you feel they aren't important. Thus, you are not living *for* yourself, but *in spite* of yourself.

People with poor self-esteem often rely on how they are doing in the present to determine how they feel about themselves. They need positive external experiences to counteract the negative feelings and thoughts that constantly plague them. Even then, the good feeling can be temporary.

THREE Faces of Low Self-Esteem

Most of us have an image of what low self-esteem looks or feels like, but it is not always so easy to recognize. There are numerous faces that are related to low self-esteem, but here are the three most common faces that low self-esteem may wear:

The Impostor: Acts happy and successful, but is really terrified of failure. The Impostor lives with the constant fear that she or he will be "found out", and needs continuous successes to maintain the mask of positive self-esteem, which may lead to problems with perfectionism, procrastination, competition, and burn-out.

The Rebel: Acts like the opinions or good will of others, especially people who are important or powerful, don't matter. The rebel lives with constant anger about not feeling "good enough", as well as continuously needing to prove that others' judgments and criticisms don't hurt, which may lead to problems like blaming others excessively, breaking rules or laws, or fighting authority.

The Loser: Acts helpless and unable to cope with the world, and waits for someone to come to the rescue. The loser uses self-pity or indifference as a shield against fear of taking responsibility for changing his or her life. The loser also looks constantly to others for guidance, which can lead to such problems as lacking assertiveness skills, under-achievement, and excessive reliance on others in relationships.

Sadly, a major problem with the self-esteem of women is the opinions of other women. Instead of fully supporting, complimenting, and boosting another women's spirits, women can be mean-spirited. Back biting, gossip, and cruel remarks seem to run rampant with women friends, family, and colleagues. If you find yourself in a situation with another woman that is detrimental to your own sense of self-worth and self-esteem, find a way to resolve the situation. Perhaps all it takes is speaking your feelings to a friend who is saying hurtful things, or to a co-worker who always points out the negative aspects of your work. Quite often, these individuals suffer from low self-esteem as well, and use a defensive or derisive attitude in order to compensate. Be mindful of this behavior next time your friends, family, or co-workers are discussing another woman, and be careful not to fall into this negative trap or mindset. By setting a good example, you will influence others, in addition to helping your own self-esteem.

"Remember, no one can make you feel inferior without your consent."
—Eleanor Roosevelt

Self-Esteem Has an Impact on All Areas of a Woman's Life Work

Behaviors learned during the school years are likely to carry over into the work world. Average girls in school are often ignored, neither reprimanded nor praised. They learn that if they do well in school, it is due to luck or hard work, not because they are capable or smart. When girls perceive that they are not good at science and math (in particular), their sense of self-esteem and aspiration for a career decline. A school culture that values the abilities and skills of individuals over competition between genders is more encouraging for girls.

Psychological well-being is positively related to the kind of roles and number of roles a person occupies. In the business world, a common method for raising personal value is in diversification – or having many skills and many acquaintances. A woman whose entire life has revolved around one person or one job may find herself and her esteem tied to this role without other outlets or options. Some researchers have found that a woman's salary is directly affected by her self-esteem.

No matter how much women love work, most women feel that good personal relationships such as friendships, marriages, or children are critical to having a balanced life. The struggle for balance between work and relationships can sometimes leave a woman feeling like a failure at both. Advancing a career usually does mean working long hours, bringing work home, and giving work the emotional energy that a woman could otherwise focus on relationships with family and friends.

Relationships

Women often are nurturing, all-giving persons, often sacrificing self over others. These actions tie women's self-worth intricately to how successful they are in relationships. Women often confuse being needed with being loved. This kind of socialization creates beliefs that the more you give, the more you get, and finds women putting others' needs above their own.

This viewpoint results in many women draining all of their personal energy and resources on others. Without replenishment, reciprocation, or appreciation for constant giving, the positive internal sense of fulfillment that was achieved through giving breaks down, and thoughts such as, "I must be doing something wrong" or "What is wrong with me?" take over.

Health

A number of health problems can be traced to low self-esteem, including eating disorders, substance abuse, depression and suicide. Some researchers (Sanford &

Donovan) have found that women have socially learned to listen to their physicians, as opposed to listening to their own body signals. This may erode a woman's belief in their own bodies and their own knowledge about themselves.

The majority of all women have some sort of issues with their body or physical appearance. Regardless of how beautiful we are, there is always a voice of dissent regarding one or more physical attributes. Even the women society deems beautiful have issues with their bodies, which is often spotlighted in the media. World famous models and actresses agonize over their weight, height, or looks, just like every other woman on the face of the earth. Instead of looking at yourself in a harsh, negative light, turn your attitude around. Think about your positive attributes, instead of ones you wish you could change. Use these positive attributes to your advantage. Instead of wishing you could wear certain types of clothing, embrace the styles that fit and flatter your body. Self-esteem is one of the best things any woman can possess, and it makes her look better in the eyes of everyone else, and in Gods eyes! *You are fearfully and wonderfully made.* (Psalm 139:14).

Do not fall into the trap of thinking material items can make you feel better about yourself. Quite often women tend to indulge themselves on extravagant or expensive items that they believe will boost their self-esteem. A designer pair of shoes or expensive purse will not fix what is wrong on the inside. No matter what you purchase, that shopping spree you just indulged in will most likely cause yourself greater self-esteem woes. It is a vicious cycle, feeling poorly about yourself, making outrageous purchases, then feeling even worse about yourself due to the surmounting bills and needless items. Instead of heading to your local mall, hit the library and check out the self-help section. You may find a book that has a great starting point for boosting your self-esteem. Money cannot buy you love or happiness, and it cannot buy you self-esteem!

Steps to a Better Self-Esteem

Before you can begin to improve your self-esteem, you must first believe that you can change it. Change doesn't necessarily happen quickly or easily, but it can happen. You are not powerless! Once you have accepted, or are at least willing to entertain the possibility that you are not powerless, there are three steps you can take to begin to change your self-esteem:

STEP 1. Begin to challenge the negative messages of the critical inner voice. Rebutting your critical inner voice is an important first step, but not enough. Since our self-esteem is in part due to how others have treated us in the past, the second step to more healthy self-esteem is equally important.

STEP 2. Begin to treat yourself as a worthwhile person. Start to challenge past negative experiences or messages by nurturing and caring for yourself in ways that show that you are valuable, competent, deserving and loveable. Some nurturing components to self-nurturing for building up your self-esteem can be practicing basic self-care, planning fun and relaxing things for yourself, rewarding yourself for your accomplishments, reminding yourself of your strength and achievements, forgiving yourself when you don't do all you have planned, and self-nurturing, even when you don't feel you deserve it.

STEP 3. Remember that self-esteem is the value we place on ourselves. Enhancing and repairing your self-esteem is the best thing you can do for your health and personal recovery. Self-esteem determines how you live. It determines how you talk, how you handle your relationships, what career you choose, what kind of lifestyle you create, and how you think, feel and act.

Keep a positive outlook on life and you will lead a positive life. Break away from negative influences, and work to surround yourself with positive individuals who will positively influence your life.

You are a great person! So many people feel this way about you, and it's time you should feel good about yourself, as well!

ABOUT THE AUTHOR

Daphne C. Ferguson-Young, DDS, MSPH

Dr. Ferguson-Young received her DDS degree and MSPH degree from Meharry Medical College. She also completed a General Practice Residency certificate program at Meharry Medical College.

Most of Dr. Ferguson-Young's professional career has been dedicated to working with individuals who have limited access to healthcare. She worked for over thirteen years at Matthew Walker Community Health Center. Dr. Ferguson-Young was in private practice before accepting a faculty appointment at Meharry Medical College, School of Dentistry. She also is a contract dentist with the Indian Health Service where she has had the opportunity to provide dental services to the Sioux Tribe in North Dakota. Dr. Ferguson-Young also serves in the USAR as a Major and was deployed to Iraq in 2004. Her tour of duty gave her the opportunity to provide dental services to Iranian detainees as well as to the American servicemen and servicewomen.

Dr. Ferguson-Young is currently an Assistant Professor in the Department of Restorative Dentistry where she teaches 2nd, 3rd, and 4th year dental students both pre clinically and clinically.

She is very active in several dental professional, academic, and community activities where she serves in several leadership capacities. Dr. Ferguson-Young is active with Capital City Dental Society, PanTN Dental Association and the National Dental Association. She currently is a member of the Mathew Walker Community Health Center Governing Board. Recently, she was selected to participate in the first National Dental Society-GlaxoKline Smith Speakers' Bureau.

Dr, Ferguson-Young has presented several professional presentations on the local, state, national and international level. She has been the recipient of several teaching awards.

Dr. Daphne C. Ferguson-Young continues to dedicate her professional life as an advocate and activist for access to quality healthcare for all individuals.

Contact
Dr. Daphne C. Ferguson-Young
2120 Lebanon Pike #38
Nashville, TN 37210
(615) 889-7760
dajayou@bellsouth.net

FOURTEEN

MARCHING TO THE BEAT OF YOUR OWN DRUM

By Dr. Daphne Young

"Trust yourself, then you will know how to live"
—Wolfgang von Goethe

In today's world, we are constantly bombarded by the media, via television and print, telling us how we should look. But, life is so much more than a facade we wear on the outside. We, as women, are so much more then the color of our hair, the clothes that we wear, and the number on that weigh-in scale.

Some of us grew up in an era where choices to decide whether we wanted a career or not were made for us. AND, if we wanted to pursue a career, we were navigated toward careers or "jobs" that were considered women's work. But, this goes beyond careers, this is about who we are as people, as individuals, as women. This is about our confidence, our self-respect and our self-esteem.

Joan Didion tells us, "To free us from the expectations of others, to give us back to ourselves, there lies the great singular power of self-respect." It is the respect that we have for ourselves, individually, which allows us to explore who we are and what our gifts and talents are. We cannot and should not be defined by someone else's definition of our own being. We cannot and should not be defined by what someone else thinks our talents and gifts are. We cannot and should not be defined by someone else's beliefs of how we should live our life.

So, where do you start to discover what you want in life and what your gifts are? First, write down **everything** that you truly enjoy doing, such as reading, writing, drawing, helping others, traveling, talking, solving problems, shopping, decorating, experimenting with make-up, acting, singing……you get the picture. Now remember, you don't have to be an expert in any of these activities, you just need to enjoy doing them. These are activities that make YOU feel good, and bring a smile to YOUR face. They can be activities that you share with others, or just something that you do for yourself.

Next, write down those activities or talents that someone else has told you that you seem to have a natural gift for.

Activities That YOU Enjoy	Activities at Which OTHERS Say You're Talented

How does the first list compare to the second list?

I am sure that there are a couple of activities that are the same on both lists. Did you surprise yourself? Are you discovering something new about yourself today? This is exciting!

According to e.e. cummings, "We do not believe in ourselves until someone reveals that what is deep inside us is valuable, worth listening to, worthy of our trust, sacred to our touch. Once we believe in ourselves, we can risk the curiosity, wonder, spontaneous delight, or any experience that reveals the human spirit." However, keep in mind that these individuals in your close inner circle are people who truly care about you, and see you as the beautiful, talented, caring individual that you are. Dr. Nathan Branden states, "The tragedy is that so many people look for self-confidence and self-respect everywhere except within themselves. And so, they fail in their search."

Now, if you are going to march to the positive beat of your own drum, you have to be sure that the messages that you give yourself every day are positive and encouraging.

Create a mantra for yourself, such as, "I am a unique individual who is beautiful inside and out. I am strong….. spiritually, emotionally, mentally and physically. I am talented, caring, giving and forgiving. I am worthy of respect. I am worthy of success."

Create your own mantra:

_____

_____

Another component for being able to march to the beat of your own drum is <u>self-acceptance.</u> The famous, formidable, late First Lady, Eleanor Roosevelt, reminds us, "No one can make you feel inferior without your permission." Also, to paraphrase Les Brown, the renowned motivator speaker, "What anybody else thinks of us doesn't make it real or true." You need to embrace yourself, hug yourself, and accept yourself.

Believe me, there is not one perfect human being in this world. People do a good job of camouflaging their shortcomings, or areas of perceived imperfections.

List the areas that you like about yourself:

1. _____
2. _____
3. _____
4. _____
5. _____
6. _____

Be determined to achieve. The possible may seem impossible from where you are in life, right now. Maybe you think that your dream to achieve a goal is out of reach, or that you have missed your opportunity, due to circumstances beyond your control. Maybe you are afraid of failure. Do you know that much of the successes that we enjoy in life today came after numerous failures? Take, for instance, something as seemingly simple as the light bulb. It took Thomas Edison years and many, many tries before he was successful. Albert Einstein is quoted as saying, "Anyone who has never made a mistake has never tried anything new." Don't fear the unknown to achieve a goal.

As the retired Chicago teacher, Marva Collins knows, "Success doesn't come to you, you go to it!"

List those activities and goals that you reached and feel great success:

- _____
- _____
- _____
- _____
- _____
- _____
- _____
- _____

Do you now realize how many times you have been marching to the beat of your own drum? Do you agree with the noted Carlyle Thomas that, "Nothing builds self-esteem and self-confidence like accomplishment?" Maybe this is your first opportunity to really write down all of your accomplishments, and be able to step back and say " not bad".

As a daughter, sister, mother, aunt, civic volunteer, grandmother, etc., there are people looking to you to set the example. Sometimes how you handle life is being observed from afar. You can be a positive or negative influence without your knowledge.

Fred Rogers, affectionately known as Mr. Rogers, put it so clearly when he said, "If only you could sense how important you are to the lives of those you meet; how important you can be to people you may never dream of. There is something of yourself that you leave at every meeting of another person."

You have been given the melody to beat the rhythm of YOUR drum. In review, they are: talents, self-esteem, belief in yourself, determination, perseverance, self-approval, self-acceptance, and last but definitely not least, self-respect.

Play your drums loudly with the pride of the Queen that you are. For Harvey Fienstein tells us to, "Never be bullied into silence. Never allow yourself to be made a victim. Accept no one's definition of your life; define yourself."

What goals do you what to achieve in the next year, while marching to the beat of your own drum?

1. _____

2. _____

3. _____

4. _____

5. _____

What is your roadmap to get there?

1. _____
2. _____
3. _____
4. _____
5. _____

Who are your mentors?

1. _____
2. _____
3. _____
4. _____
5. _____

To march to the beat of your own drum is one of the gifts that all women should embrace.

Never hesitate to ask for advice along the way, but be certain that whatever drum beat you choose, that it is one from your own heart.

Reading Resources

Self-Esteem and Empowerment for Women (The Professional Woman Library)

Loving Yourself More: 101 Meditations on Self-Esteem for Women

Dancing on the Glass Ceiling – Find Your True Strength, Activate Your Vision and Get What You Really Want Out of Life by Candy Deemer and Nancy Fredricks

Bring It On – Women Embracing Midlife by Christine Carter Schaap

Women Changing Work by Patricia Lunneborg

Notes:

ABOUT THE AUTHOR

MICHELÉ LAWLIS

Michelé E. Lawlis founded The DIVA Institute, Inc. (TDI) in February of 2005 to pursue her passion of restoring hope and purpose into the lives of young women and single (unwed) mothers. TDI is an independent provider of customized personal & professional development services to promote self-empowerment, leadership & community engagement. After rising above her own struggles with childhood adversity and single parenting, Ms. Lawlis was called to devote her efforts toward empowering women to challenge negative stereotypes by becoming visionary managers of their lives, families & careers. She encourages young women to focus on reaching their highest potential and building healthy relationships before pursuing marriage and motherhood. Ms. Lawlis also asserts that with honest self-analysis, faith, determination and adequate resources single mothers can overcome internal barriers and external influences to make a strong impact on our communities.

TDI's mission is to educate, enlighten and empower women by elevating the mind & spirit toward self-love, purpose-driven living and collective awareness; creating a network of visionaries who are motivated toward personal action that will effect positive change in their communities. As a certified trainer on women's issues and professional coach, Ms. Lawlis has created a reputation for TDI as the trainer of choice for many single mothers. The DIVA process and non-traditional approaches guide them on a journey of unleashing self-contained power to reach their personal and professional development goals. Her compassion, willingness to be transparent, and candor instantly create an environment which embraces those who are ready to move beyond their circumstances. As a highly sought-after trainer and public speaker, Ms. Lawlis has inspired many to overcome adversity and unleash their inner DIVA (Divine Insight & Vision in Action) against cycles of nihilism & dysfunction. She is noted for delivering thought-provoking keynotes, which have motivated thousands to re-evaluate their commitments to self, family & community in order to live according to purpose. As Ms. Lawlis is equally concerned with the competencies of those in position to provide resources to the women TDI serves, customized sensitivity training is also provided as an option for interested parties. Service-providers and clients of faith and community-based organizations, government agencies, schools, colleges and universities throughout the United States have been inspired by TDI seminars and presentations.

Ms. Lawlis is an appointed member of the International Advisory Board and Speakers Bureau of The Professional Woman Network (PWN). In addition to personal experience as a working single mother, Ms. Lawlis has a diverse professional background in family law, city government, social services, women's employment rights, non-profit grant administration, workforce development and conflict mediation. A strong advocate of servant leadership, she has also served on various boards & committees for organizations promoting diversity, youth development, higher education and community engagement. Ms. Lawlis is an active member of several professional organizations, and has been recognized by Who's Who associations, public school systems and community organizations for her dedication to empowering women and youth from diverse backgrounds to effect social change through purposeful living.

Ms. Lawlis holds a degree in Political Science from the University of Louisville, and is a certified trainer on diversity, women's issues & youth development. She is available on an international basis to train, consult & keynote.

Contact:
The DIVA Institute, Inc.
P.O. Box 161371
Louisville, KY 40256
(502) 290-4406
www.TheDIVAInstitute.com

FIFTEEN

PRETTY IS AS PRETTY DOES: LIVING A LIFE OF PURPOSE

By Michelé Lawlis

"Women, if the soul of the nation is to be saved, I believe that you must become its soul." —Coretta Scott King

Mrs. Martin Luther King, Jr. retired from this world on January 30, 2006, but her memory lives on as one of beauty, strength and purpose. Understanding that she was not only married to the man, but to the cause, she continued the struggle for civil rights and social justice in the United States after the tragic assassination of her husband. Mrs. King also spoke frequently about the importance of women serving as advocates on behalf of their families and communities. By issuing the call for women to rise up as the saving grace for our nation,

Coretta Scott King encouraged us to become women of great depth and spirit. Although she was striking to the eye, many have recalled that her beauty did not rest solely in her physical appearance. She possessed the kind of grace, wisdom and love for all people that embraced the very soul of those in her presence.

How do we become the soul of the nation? I believe it starts with discovering the truth of who you are at the very core of your being. "Soul" is defined as the principle, or basic source of life, feeling, thought and action in humans. If I asked you to describe yourself, you would more than likely begin to provide me with a list of physical attributes. You might begin with your height, weight, hair length, eye color, etc. However, if I asked you to describe yourself from the soul, what would be your response? Your soul is the place where your true essence resides. Your soul is the place where you find the answers to questions like, "Who am I?", "Why do I exist?", and "Where do I go from here?" Ultimately, your soul is the place wherein lies your passion, potential and purpose.

As a young girl, I remember spending a warm summer afternoon on the front porch of Aunt Ivy's. My cousin and I were seated at her feet and swapping stories about the happenings of our young lives. She listened intently as we told her about school, our peers, and some of the drama that existed in our little junior high worlds. We obsessed about the competitive and bossy nature of little girls who did not want to be our friends. We complained about the nuisance, yet unexplainable excitement, of little boys who teased us about being pretty and made fun of our physical appearance, while at the same time asking for our telephone numbers. At our wits end, we tried desperately to figure out how to manage all of the confusion. As we chatted away, I remember thinking to myself that our experiences must require some serious intervention if Aunt Ivy was so determined to listen. However, I grew to understand that Aunt Ivy was simply waiting for the right moment to share a wisdom and instruction that would encourage us to look beyond the surface of ourselves, and life in general. Twenty years later, I can still hear the words as if she were sitting right next to me, "Ladies, just remember that pretty is as pretty does." You may recognize this familiar saying as one passed down from generations in your own family. It simply refers to the realization that outer beauty is nice, but possessing inner beauty is most important. Your soul is the substance of your inner beauty, and the purpose within is your power. Developing your inner beauty will improve your life and our world, for that which exists on the inside always impacts the outside.

Society has placed a great deal of pressure on women to conform to its ideals of female worth. The negative images of women in the entertainment and music industries portray us as sex objects and disorderly divas stalked as pawns for ratings and Reality TV shows. Film and fashion industries suggest that beauty is determined by your weight, hairstyle, clothes and car. Women are less often characterized as pretty or graceful, but more as glamorous, sexy and voluptuous. As the rates continue to climb for divorce, single female-headed households, sexually transmitted diseases, depression, and domestic and sexual abuse against women, we recognize all of this feeds a continuous cycle that degrades the female and strips her of the respect for being a worthy and meaningful contributor to our world. Some school-aged girls, when asked what comes to mind when they think of the word pretty, provide the anticipated responses regarding physical attributes, but also associate characteristics like good attitude, personality and behavior. Despite our understanding of the aforementioned, as a society in general we place less emphasis on the development of character than on physical appearance. The multi-billion dollar industries of cosmetics and plastic surgery indicate that many women are literally buying into the idea that they alone are not good enough.

How can you rise above these misperceptions to increase your value and live a life of purpose? I submit to you that you are more than what you see. In order to live a life of purpose, it is not only important for you to know who you are, but for you to celebrate YOU. If you do not feel good about yourself, it will be extremely difficult for you to recognize your value. Living a life of purpose requires you to be aware of that which makes you unique. It requires understanding there is a contribution for this world that can be made by no one else but you! You were created for this purpose, and it will not become manifest until you bring it to pass. Your purpose is not linked to what someone else has, feels, or portrays. It is all about you and what you do to impact the lives of others. Purpose is born in the soul, resides within, and radiates throughout. Remember, pretty is as pretty does, so let us begin with a "pretty analysis".

The following exercises will guide you on a journey of defining what pretty means to you based upon your self-perception and personal goals. You will have an opportunity to 1) conduct an honest assessment of who you are today, 2) establish goals for personal growth and development, and 3) start pursuing your purpose. At the conclusion of the exercises, you will have a customized roadmap to continue developing your inner beauty.

Personality

Your personality displays your essential character. In the field of psychology, it is defined as the sum total of the physical, mental, emotional, and social characteristics of an individual.

Do you feel you have a pleasing personality? If so, what aspects make it so?

_____
_____

The personality/ego can overshadow the radiance of the soul if the two are not in concert. In his book *Silent Power,* Stuart Wilde refers to our ability to develop a silent power or charisma that gradually develops around us. This power is called the etheric or subtle body, an electromagnetic body of energy. Wilde advises us to, "See the world as energy, and become responsible for *your* energy."

How do others define your personality?

_____
_____

Identify one or two characteristics of your personality you would like to improve. What steps will you take to do so?

_____
_____

Relationships

We are born with an inherent desire to connect with others. Human interaction is as essential to our existence as water is to fish. We may temporarily be able to breathe without it, but our capacity to survive is restricted. Eventually, we must be reunited to that which refreshes and restores us, or face a slow and painful demise. It is important to note that the state of your relationships is equally critical to your survival. Relationships that are supportive and nurturing will confirm your feelings of value, and benefit your personal growth by challenging you to reach your full potential. Unhealthy relationships will force you to compromise your personal values, lower your self-esteem, and lock you into a cycle of limited growth and potential. You will not feel good about yourself if you allow others to disrespect and mistreat you physically, emotionally, verbally and/or spiritually. You cannot operate in purpose and receive spiritual clarity if you remain imprisoned by the limited views and intentions of others. Whether considering co-workers, friends, acquaintances and/or family, know that your self-perception is vulnerable to your relationships. As you continue to grow, you will place more emphasis on the quality of your relationships vs. the quantity.

Some of you may experience difficulty in analyzing your intimate relationships. However, I encourage you to be honest with yourself about the impact of your interactions. Identifying a relationship as being unhealthy for you does not directly indicate the other individual is a "bad" person. It only suggests there is an element of your interactions that is not compatible with your true self. Acknowledging this can set both of you on a path toward emotional healing and freedom.

You must acquire the faith and strength necessary to overcome unhealthy family patterns, as well. "Every time you change or release a negative family pattern, you create a new identity" according to Denise Linn, author of *Four Acts of Personal Power*. As we discovered earlier, your purpose is not dependent upon the expectations and requirements of others. Families are often the most resistant to change. You have been the same person your entire life, so they expect nothing less, and certainly nothing more, than for you to go along with the status quo. Our family identity is usually drastically different from our public image. A high-powered and controlled CEO in corporate America may become the "baby-girl" who pounces on the last scoop of her grandfather's bread stuffing to beat out a swarm of uncles at Thanksgiving dinner. A justice of the courts may be labeled the "most wanted" family team member because of a winning streak in the card games of spades or taboo. A store clerk may be considered the family planner and organizer, or the glue that holds everyone together. Roles such as these may not present a threat, but may serve to keep these women grounded, and provide comfort from the demands of their positions. As you continue to grow in spirit and purpose, your healthy relationships will be nurtured by your increased confidence and strength of presence. However, if any of your relationship roles, or the demands of such, create any level of discomfort, they must be re-evaluated. Failure to do so and establish sufficient boundaries will negatively impact your emotional health and burden your spirit.

This exercise will guide you in conducting a cost-benefit analysis of your relationships. Consider the benefits of those with whom you share a healthy and supportive relationship. What do you gain from their presence? How do those with whom you share an unhealthy relationship leave you deficient and inadequate?

Name	Relationship	Explain Cost/Benefit (C/B)

What boundaries would you like to establish for those relationships that cost?

Name	Boundary

What steps can you take within the next (30) days to begin setting those boundaries?

Boundary	Steps

How can your current or future mate support you in maintaining your sense of value and purpose?

1. _____

2. _____

3. _____

How can your family members do the same?

1. _____
2. _____
3. _____

What steps can you take to be more nurturing and supportive with those who you share healthy relationships?

1. _____
2. _____
3. _____

Excellence

Do you exhibit excellence in everything you do? Think carefully before you answer this question, as excellence requires a total commitment from you to do the best you can with what you have. "Life with meaning and purpose does exist, but it's the result of conscious choices," according to Denise Brown, author of *Work with Who You Are*. Again I ask, do you feel that excellence is your personal standard, or is it possible that you could put forth more effort in reaching your personal, family or career goals. Do you carry yourself and dress in a manner that suggests you respect and appreciate yourself? Do you take advantage of opportunities to expand your knowledge and experiences? Do others feel inspired to do or be better when you are around? I caution you to note that excellence does not require perfection, physical or otherwise. Make no mistake that pursuing a new standard of beauty through purposeful living will require integrity, stamina, and endurance that commands the very best of who you are. Prepare yourself now by raising your standard.

Who do you consider to be a role model(s) of excellence? Why?

1. _____

because: _____

2. _____

because: _____

3. _____

because: _____

In what area(s) of your life do you want to begin exhibiting more excellence (personal/family/career)? How?

1. _____

2. _____

3. _____

4. _____

5. _____

Time

As mentioned previously, you are not expected to be perfect as you journey toward purpose. A few bumps in the road every now and then will actually help to build your character and strength. However, you must not become sidetracked when things do not work out as you may have intended. I have learned that every life experience, good and bad, holds value. Failed relationships, past disappointments, grief from lost loved ones can leave us all feeling suspended in time, and questioning whether or not we made all of the right decisions. Courageously ask for insight that reveals the lesson. The Divine will send a reply that increases our wisdom, propels us past painful repeats, and reveals its purpose. Appreciate every new day that you are given an opportunity to be the best of who you are. Life can pass you by in the blink of an eye. *"Your assignment is to be present, passionate and purposeful."* —Dr. Nicole LaBeach, *A Woman's True Purpose*.

What ritual can I create to celebrate the blessing of each new day?

Talents

Your natural talents are also an indicator of purpose, as we are reminded that purpose relates to how you impact others. Have you ever felt the heart of a singer, the enthusiasm of a dancer, or the passion of an artist? As they experience the ease of performing in the manner for which they were created, you cannot escape the illumination of their immense satisfaction. You know there is nothing else they would rather do. They possess an inner glow and confidence that could inspire any amateur to attempt their feats.

What natural talent(s) do you possess?

1. _____

2. _____

3. _____

How do you feel when you are engaged in displaying this talent? Why?

1. _____

2. _____

3. _____

How can you benefit others by sharing more of this talent?

1. _____

2. _____

3. _____

Your Passion

In this exercise, you will begin to discover the elements of your purpose. Remember, you have evaluated your personality, relationships, standard of excellence, and time and talent(s). Now you must complete the final step to redefining beauty for yourself. Once you have done so, your personal road map will be complete.

What do I possess a passion for doing?

1. _____

2. _____

3. _____

I believe others can benefit from me sharing that passion in the following ways:

1. _____

2. _____

3. _____

I choose to make the indicated improvements to the following areas of my life within (30) days in order to prepare myself for purposeful living:

Personality

1. _____

2. _____

Relationships

1. _____

2. _____

Excellence

1. _____

2. _____

Time

1. _____

2. _____

Talent(s)

1. _____

2. _____

Your Passion

1. _____

2. _____

I wish you the best as you embark upon your journey of purpose. I look forward to the impact your soul will have as you share it with the rest of the world. Celebrate who you are, with an intensity that motivates others to do the same. And finally, remember that pretty is as pretty does, for nothing is more beautiful than a woman who lives according to purpose.

Notes:

ABOUT THE AUTHOR

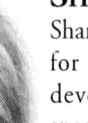

SHARYN LYNN YONKMAN

Sharyn Lynn Yonkman is the founder and principal consultant for Lynn Consulting Group, a personal and professional development training organization. Lynn Consulting specializes in career advancement skills for the professional woman, helping her in achieving personal excellence. As a passionate advocate of women's Self-empowerment and life balance issues, Sharyn offers special expertise in dealing with transition and change in the workplace, as well as programs designed for those of the baby boomer generation.

As former CFO of several high profile retail and hospitality companies, Ms. Yonkman has gained valuable in depth financial and managerial experience in the corporate community providing the knowledge for cost effective solutions for todays business challenges. Programs available include: Interactive Sensitivity and Diversity Training: Superior Customer Service in Retail and Hospitality; and Handling Conflict Fear and Transition.

One on one individual life balance coaching is available in addition to group sessions. Highly customized curriculum is offered to meet your specific organizational needs. Ms. Yonkman is a Co-author of *Remarkable Women*, an anthology project with Marci Shimoff of "*The Secret*", and actress Jennifer O'Neil. Additionally, she is an author in several of the PWP library books, including *Becoming The Professional Woman* in which she addresses overcoming fear ; *Overcoming the Superwoman Syndrome,; You're on Stage! Image Etiquette, Branding & Style,* and *A Woman's Survival guide for Overcoming Obstacles, Transition and Change.* She is currently completing a self-help book for baby boomer women facing the challenges of moving from the first act of life to the second, and would love to hear input from her fellow boomers on how they feel. Please contact her at the email provided below.

Author, trainer, motivational speaker, and life balance coach, Ms. Yonkman is available internationally to help the individual or organization with their professional and personal developmental needs.

Contact:
Sharyn Lynn Yonkman
PO Box 1266
Ventura, Ca 93002
805.677.3117
www.protrain.net
Email: lynnconsult@yahoo.com

SIXTEEN

THE PORTRAYAL OF WOMEN IN THE MEDIA

By Sharyn Lynn Yonkman

How does one begin to go beyond the body and develop inner beauty (as the title of this book advocates) with the constant barrage of media telling us to do otherwise? When you are repeatedly told that beauty is something that comes from without, how does one go within? It is a serious challenge, one that I ask you to take on as I endeavor to provide you with some insights and ammunition for this task. Are you up to the challenge? If so, please join me and read on.

"Although beauty may be in the eye of the beholder, the feeling of being beautiful exists solely in the mind of the beheld."—Martha Beck

Portrayal or Betrayal?

How does the media portray women? In my view, the media does not so much portray women, as much as it betrays women. This betrayal takes many forms. A few include:

- The objectification of women as sex symbols and its subsequent influence of sexual attitudes and male dominance

- The normalizing of the abnormal by preaching the doctrine of unattainable beauty

- The encouragement of an atmosphere of dangerous weight preoccupation

The media should set the tone to value women for their abilities, rather than merely value their physical attributes. Unfortunately, the message being delivered by the media is often that it is more important to be thin, young, or to have large breasts than it is to be capable, authentic, or successful.

Images of the female body are everywhere selling virtually everything. Advertising is the economic lifeblood of the mass media. All products continue to exist because there is a market for them. By presenting an ideal body image that is extremely difficult (at best) to achieve and/or maintain, the beauty and diet industries are assured of continued growth, and thereby increased profits.

Beyond the world of advertising, commerce, and pop culture, women still fare poorly. Serious journalism shows little interest in women's issues and challenges on a global basis. Even in their portrayal of the many women who are in notable leadership roles in various arenas, often more importance and attention is given to the women's personal affairs and her appearance rather than her accomplishments.

The lack of women in the mostly male dominated world of journalism contributes to this demeaning representation in the press. If there is to be a meaningful account of women's issues in journalism, more women need to be encouraged to join the profession, even though it is traditionally a "good old boys club", and therefore a difficult world for women to enter. One hopes as more women break into this world, especially at management decision-making levels, the lack of proper attention to women's voices will be addressed and they will be at long last heard.

Go Within Exercise
Take a moment to reflect upon what you think about the portrayal of women in the media. What is your reaction?
1. _____
2. _____

- Do you feel betrayed or empowered by the messages it sends?
1. _____
2. _____

"Beauty is not caused. It is." —Emily Dickinson

Women as Objects
The objectification of women in the media is detrimental in several ways. It is common in the media to portray the notion that as women we can control our social value just by controlling our appearance. She is conditioned to view her face as a mask and her body as an object.

The message is that the female body is an object, and one that must be perfect, every part of it. Constantly objectified by the media, a woman learns to objectify herself and judge her total worth by the media "worthiness" of her body parts.

No matter what the product, "sex sells." Sex in advertising is demeaning and objectifying. Many of the provocative poses used to sell products are adapted from pornography and these overtly suggestive poses add to the notion that male approval is the most important measure of a women's worth.

Additionally, ads that objectify women encourage men to think of women as unequal and/or inferior. When a woman is turned into an object, it is the first step toward justifying violence against her. This is so because men would not so easily oppress someone they perceived as an equal. It is harder to be violent against an equal than an inferior.

"Nonsense and beauty have close connection." —E.M. Forster

Self-Improvement or Self-Destruction?

The barrage of messages the media delivers about beauty, with its emphasis on thinness and youth, tells "ordinary" women that they are inadequate and forever in need of improvement. Since no one is flawless (not even the air- brushed cover girls), and everyone ages, the image portrayed by media is artificial and unrealistic. Perhaps most disturbing is the fact that media images of female beauty are unattainable for all but a very few women. Because of this, women will go to great lengths to manipulate and change their appearance to adhere to this image.

This idea of perfection is misleading. Naturally, we cannot relate to the air brushed cover girl perfection, so we try to emulate, instead. We disappear as authentic women when we remodel our bodies surgically to meet those externally imposed standards of female beauty.

The message the media consistently delivers is that perfection is not only attainable, but also mandatory. This message results in body shame. Women who are insecure about their bodies are more likely to buy beauty products, diet aids, and expensive plastic surgery procedures. That is exactly what the advertisers want you to do, so the unrealistic images keep coming. We like to tell ourselves that advertising does not affect us, but we find ourselves buying the "dream image", as well as the product.

The media should reflect the diversity that defines the contemporary woman. That includes women of all shapes, sizes, races, ethnicities, ages, as well as a broad range of occupations, activities and life-styles. This omission, by the media, of natures many variations in physical appearance, contributes to the current prevalence of body image shame. This shame can be transformed into much of the dangerous plastic surgery done and eating disorders.

Women and Food

Through the ages, women have always been linked to food. Our very biology provides that basic link and our role as nest builders and nurturers further enforces the connection. Men often refer to us as "dishes", "honey", "tomatoes", "sugar", "peaches", and "arm candy".

How often have you seen a magazine cover declaring the recipe within for the ultimate, decadent chocolate dessert, and right next to this declaration is the announcement for the newest diet fad so you might lose those ten pounds now?

Often times, women's magazines have articles urging us that if we could just lose those last fifteen or twenty pounds, we would have the perfect life. And it is not only magazine articles and print ads that teach this doctrine. Movies and television reinforce the importance of thinness as a measure of a woman's value. Often, heavier actresses are either not used, or when they are, their characters receive negative comments about their bodies and are the brunt of cruel jokes.

One must ask why these unhealthy standards of beauty are being imposed on women, when the vast majority of women are larger than any of the models or actresses being used? How are we to relate? Unfortunately, when we cannot relate, we often try to emulate, and thus begins the downward spiral of eating disorders.

Vulnerability of Younger Women

One of the most insidious betrayals by the media is perpetrated on girls and young women. Adolescent girls and young women are particularly vulnerable to media hype, due to their lack of experience and impressionable minds. They are at a time in their lives when they are learning their values, developing their identities, and are sensitive to peer pressure.

From a very early age, women are bombarded with images that are unrealistic. One of the most famous (or infamous) examples is the Barbie doll. Over the last several decades, Barbie has become a major icon for young girls. In addition to her unattainable measurements, Barbie sends the message that a woman's time is best spent shopping and talking on the phone. Girls begin to stereotype the ideal female as the pretty, blond, slim, big breasted and vapid model that Barbie represents.

Continually bombarded with unrealistic media images of overly thin, perfect female bodies, young women are especially vulnerable to eating disorders. These images are also linked to depression and loss of self-esteem. The numbers of women and girls who seek to emulate that underweight body image is epidemic, and they can suffer devastating health consequences, as a result.

Another disturbing media image is one portrayed by the music industry. In lyrics and videos, women are represented as sexual objects. The song lyrics portray women as "bitches" and "hos", and in the music videos women are often portrayed as passive sex objects for men to dominate.

Equally alarming is what children see depicted as social norms. Women are encouraged to remain little girls (passive, dependent, never to mature). The vilification of maturity is insulting to adult women, and the allusion that little girls are seductive is very dangerous to children.

What does all this say to young girls, and how does it shape their self-image?

> **WHAT YOU CAN DO TO HELP**
>
> We all have some girls and young women in our sphere of influence, and it is our responsibility to set the stage for body love, not body shame. In addition to setting a good example, you can learn more about this important issue from a group known as About-Face. This organization is devoted to a campaign entitled "Stop Starvation Imagery". Visit them at www.about-face.org.

Author's Personal Declaration

I must confess that, as a former model and recovering fashionista, I, too, was once addicted to the gospel according to Vogue, Bazaar, etc. I was fortunate, however, since I never succumbed to the pressure of going to extremes in emulating the physical constraints they portray. My affliction lent itself merely to worshipping at the alter of high fashion. That being said, I was certainly not immune to the siren song of the media. This was brought home to me a few years ago when I first noticed ads for Dove products and their 'Real Beauty" campaign. I was shocked, and somewhat horrified, by my initial reaction to these ads. The most shocking part to me was how "unreal" the real women appeared to me. Being so accustomed to seeing nothing but unrealistic perfection, when I saw a real life representation, it appeared somehow wrong or false. It was quite a wake-up call for me, and forced me to confront how the media affected my psyche by going within. I am pleased to say that the outcome of that self-reflection spurred me to want to contribute this chapter in hopes that I might help others to become self-aware and active.

The power of women to cause societal change through their actions is a force to be reckoned with. Through the ages, women have collectively used their power to right wrongs and make significant contributions to society. We should not be passive victims of advertising and media betrayal. Instead, we should work toward creating a well-informed and educated public that will not tolerate harmful advertising, and will vigorously fight against it.

"Exuberance is beauty" —William Blake

Awareness and Action

Awareness is our weapon against the media onslaught. The first step is for each of us is to become more aware of the images we are being bombarded with daily, from all sources. Consider the content of various magazines, TV shows, commercials, music, movies and video games. What do they say about women? How are women portrayed?

The following are some questions you might like to consider in raising your awareness of the messages the media delivers about women. Perhaps they can be a basis for personal reflection and research, or lead to open discussion in a group forum. Consider these:

- What should you look for in a magazine to determine how it views women?

- How do fashion trends reflect our beliefs on how women should look?

- How are race and status depicted in the media's portrayal of women?

- Does advertising effect the content of women's magazines?

Please add questions of your own.

_____
_____
_____
_____

Since advertising is all about making money, the most powerful and effective way **YOU** can make a difference is via the power of your purchasing dollars. If a product's ad is offensive, women should not buy the product. Refuse to buy the product or view the shows that continually portray women in a negative, demeaning or harmful way. You can and should boycott products whose ad campaigns promote offensive and harmful images.

Why not lend your support to magazines, movies, TV shows and products that promote the idea that women should be valued for their abilities rather than their looks? Media outlets that promote an image of healthy and strong women deserve your support, as well as those that focus on the product rather than the female body. Let these companies know that you support what they are doing, and are purchasing their products because of the way they positively portray women.

And please go one step further. Let a company know you are not purchasing their products because of their offensive advertising. Encourage others to do the same.

The following are some tips to help you do just that:

How to Write an Effective Comment Letter

1. Write it ASAP. The information will be fresh in your mind, and so will your emotional reaction to it.

2. Be specific as to the medium. For TV commercials, be sure to include time, date, and station. For articles, identify publication, issue, writer, and page. Similar information is needed for print ads, as well.

3. Write persuasively and criticize constructively. Explain your position in a clear and concise way. Focus on the issue, (not organization or individual), and be specific about what it is you object to and the reason why.

4. Suggest alternatives. If you think of an alternative image to replace the offensive one, offer it.

5. Remember to identify yourself and provide your complete contact information.

6. Remind the addressee what is at stake. You and your sphere of influence are a valuable market source for that specific media and/or product depicted. Consider a boycott of the station, publication, or product involved, and be sure to mention your intent.

7. Ask for a timely response. If not received, follow up with an additional letter or phone call.

Together, women can make a difference!

ABOUT THE AUTHOR

SHERRON SPARKS HAIN

Sherron is President and CEO of Sparks Business Institute, an end-source Training and Executive Leadership Coaching entity for high-achieving women executives in succession for CEO/COO positions.

She is in the dissertation phase of her PhD in Industrial/Organizational Psychology and has her Masters of Science Degree in Organizational Leadership.

Sherron is published writer and formerly had her own Marketing and Public Relations firm that covered a six-state area. She began her parent company, SCS, LLC in 1989 as a Public Relations, Promotions and Marketing Agency, and as the needs of her clients grew, she realized a desperate need for good business counseling and training with focused attention on the core competencies that women need to assume leadership positions.

She is host of Stop Gap - a syndicated radio show that focuses on the issues and trends of women in business. Her guests include outstanding women across the United States who are leading the effort for equality in issues that affect women, including, wage, health care, technology and education. The show is starting its second year of braodcasting.

Sherron is a member of Rotary,, SHRM, NAFE, NCDA, multiple local Chambers of Commerce and The Professional Woman Network where she holds an advisory board position.

Contact
Sherron Sparks Hain, MSOL
Sparks Business Institute
1102 N Front Street, Harrisburg, PA 17102
717-513-0011
sherron@sparksbusinessinstitute.org
www.sparksbusinessinstitute.org
www.protrain.net

SEVENTEEN

WHEN YOU'VE FALLEN OR FAILED

By Sherron Sparks Hain

Breathe…just breathe! Sometimes that's all you can do. Close your eyes and listen to the rhythm of your own breathing – it can give you peace. It can give you a constant in a world that seems to be out of control in every area. It is a small something you can begin to control again in your life. Slowly, breathe in to the slow count of five; now exhale to the slow count of five. Almost like Lamaze, only this time you are giving birth to yourself, one painful breath at a time. It is a journey, a painful transition, but a joy to hold as you cradle yourself when you have overcome the pain of your perceived failure.

Falling and Failing

It is a woman's private hell, one in which we put our practiced face and pretend that our life is ok, never letting the world know we are at the bottom of the pit. Falling. Failing. Our business may be failing. Our marriage may be a silent prison – abusive, disastrous. Our children may be involved with the wrong crowd or be caught up in a legal battle. The job we love is taken. The schooling that was going to make a difference came to an abrupt end when we were trying so hard. Kicked (dismissed is nicer) out of the church for our personal beliefs. We consider it our failure. We cover it with our smile, we cover it with our busyness, but we don't want to let people know how desperate we are, and how very badly we feel as a failure. We are the face of strength to our families; this face can show no weakness.

I speak to many women clients who repeat the same stories. These women are not always the down trodden, the abused, or the broken housewife – it also happens to very public professional women. I have been there several times myself; broken, depressed, my soul bleeding and wondering how a nice person like me, who has no ill will for anyone, can be in the depths of despair. My "Polly-Anna" world-view says it shouldn't happen to good people like me. You'd think it would happen to the dark, evil, sinister people that hurt others. How did I get here? Who, I agonized again and again, is responsible for me being in this bad place in my life? Wake up Polly Anna – **YOU DID IT TO YOURSELF!**

It is a hard lesson that many of my clients do not want to hear, nor did I. We want someone to blame. We were doing our best. It couldn't be me; it was "dog breath!" (my divorce attorney's favorite name for husbands, but the word may be substituted for bosses, etc. for a moment of comic relief.)

The empathy soothes the pain for a moment. Then, it is time to deal with it, what brought you to this day.

Look very carefully at your current situation. Ruthlessly assess why you are at this place in your life. I will provide some exercises to help you. Then, we will make a conscious effort to: change your behavior, change your choices, and change your life. You will learn to make good solid decisions and count your blessings. The secret is in your choices, your decision-making, and your gratitude. But only YOU have the power to make the change.

Decisions

If I told you that "today" you are creating the hell you will live with in five years, would you believe me? Would you make different decisions?

Well, it's true! Your life in five years will be a direct reflection of the decisions you make today. Your life today is a direct reflection of the decisions you made years ago. Don't believe it? Look at your life, examine it carefully, and go back to the decision or the 'cross road' that put you on this path to the joy filled life you are experiencing, or the despair that is slowly killing you. Go back. What was your decision at that cross road?

I am an Industrial/Organizational Psychologist who deals mainly with work and career- related issues, but I also work with many women in my practice. A lot of the women tell similar stories. It can be relationship problems affecting work, or it can be work problems affecting every aspect of their lives. It is a direct correlation as to how we are socialized.

Let's look at the example of a young woman who came to me through her work problems who was in an abusive and disastrous marriage. The following is how we retraced the steps:

"Go back.
When did it start to go wrong?

What decision did you make that took you to this point?

Did you overlook that first flash of verbal abuse and wonder where that came from? Did you decide at that point, although it was very bad, that basically he must have had a bad day, and ignore the pain in your gut, or the flashing warning. Point 1 – he got away with it. You were kind and sweet because you wanted to make a perfect marriage, and turned a blind eye to what had happened. You served him a great dinner and covered up your pain. He was rewarded for bad behavior.

The next time it came, maybe it was in the form of hateful, hurtful lies. You, of course, stood your ground, fought, and then pretended to believe that he would never lie to you. You wanted to make peace. Women are the peacekeepers. Point 2 – he got away with it. Add another point in his game.

Another time it was maybe the abusive language that came out in a fight. You wondered where that came from. He tells you that you provoked him to anger, and you know that you certainly gave as good as you got, so you accept his statement and guilt and promise not to do that again. Point 3 – he got away with it.

The next cross road decision comes when you witness his violence. This time you are afraid. He uses point three again because he got away with it last time, and you certainly don't want to provoke that again, so you remain silent. Point 4 – he got away with it. It would be embarrassing to let anyone know what is going on in your life, you are well respected by other women in your office and your peers, and so you suffer in silence.

It goes on and on. Abuse escalates unless it is stopped. But, by the time most women know they are in it, it is beyond the point of stopping it easily without help, and a marriage disintegrates."

This is a relationship pit, but it can be the same with business. Go back through the crossroad decisions in business or your personal life and retrace the steps, one by one, that happened from the decision you made at the Y in the road.

The following is an exercise you can use to examine your pivotal decisions.

Decision **You Made** at the Crossroad

Decision at Crossroads	Decision Made	Outcome You are Living With

Decision **You COULD HAVE Made** at the Crossroad

Decision at Crossroads	Decision Made	Outcome You Will Live With

1. Compare the results of the decision you made and the one you could have made. _____
_____
_____
_____

2. Could your decisions, with enough forethought, have made a difference in what you are experiencing today? _____
_____
_____
_____

3. Did you rush into it? _____
_____
_____
_____

4. Did you make a bad call? _____
_____
_____
_____

5. Did you hurt people unnecessarily with your decision? _____
_____
_____
_____

6. Can you make it up to those you have hurt? How?_____
_____
_____
_____

7. Have you paid dearly for the decision you made? _____
_____
_____
_____

8. How much longer are you going to pay? _____
_____
_____
_____

9. Do you deserve to be punished any longer for the decision made a long time ago? _____
_____
_____
_____

10. What are you going to do about it? _____
_____
_____
_____

11. Do you need some professional help to push through this? (Advice or Protection) _____
_____
_____
_____

12. How will you be different by doing this? _____
_____
_____
_____

13. Are you ready? What do you need to do before you begin? __
_____
_____
_____

Making good solid decisions is imperative for your happiness. Yet, most people, especially women, are not great decision makers because of their socialization – we are taught to play nice. We make decisions for others well, but do not make good decisions for ourselves. The following are some tips that will help you to make good decisions.

1. STOP – Stop before you make a decision and THINK! Think ahead. Many decisions are made with great passion for what is going on in front of you. You need to stop the momentum of events pushing you to decide, so you can make a solid choice that will guide your life in days to come. STOP! Do a calm analysis of the events that are pushing you. Taking the time to think it through helps prevent rash decisions.

A good friend of mine with the SBA (Small Business Administration) said there would be a lot less businesses, and business failures, if only people would take the time to think things through and to do a business plan for how it is going to affect them in the next five years.

2. GOALS – Clarify your Goals. Do you have a goal? What are your long-term goals affected by this decision? What are your short-term goals affected by this decision? Is this decision filling an immediate want or need? Is it going to affect or prevent the achievement of your other life goals?

I have a young client in her mid-twenties. Her long time goal was to get her Doctorate degree and work around the world as a Research Scientist. She is absolutely brilliant and fought hard for a Masters Degree, almost losing her long time boyfriend because he didn't want her to take time from him and their relationship. She finished, they got married, and supposedly lived happily ever after with a few minor changes until she wanted to pursue her Doctorate degree so she could get back to her dream, teach in the local university and travel. She was over qualified for the small town they lived in and couldn't find a job. She was unable to teach without her Doctorate at the University. He said NO. They had responsibilities – his new truck payment. She now works taking care of children in the local day care for minimum wage. And sometimes she cries. They have no children. She wonders where she gave up on her dreams and started living his. She doesn't know how to go about living hers anymore.

3. FACTS – Do you have the facts to make an intelligent choice? Do you know how all the ramifications of this decision are going to affect your life in the long run? Are you overlooking any important facts, due to the passion of the moment and your immediate wants and needs? Most people don't take the time to verify their assumptions. It is better to feel the pain of your false or broken assumptions before a marriage, or a job position to which you are tied. Assumptions are not facts; neither are promises. Facts have different versions and meanings among people. Clarify exactly what is meant by each fact.

4. OPINIONS – Develop your own opinions. It is ok to listen to the advice of others in making your decisions, but remember that they are formulated in the minds and from the lives of someone other than you. It may be a great opinion, but not hold true for your life. Well meaning family, friends and church members etc. feel they have the answer to your problems – they don't! Only you do. You have to go a little deeper into your gut – but you have the answer. YOUR OPINION MATTERS!

Make a list of all the facts and opinions that people are giving you, run them through your mental and heart-felt sieve. Throw away those that bring a sinking feeling to your gut – I don't care if it is your future husband, future mother in-law, future boss, preacher, Pope, etc. Listen to your body. Clarify the facts according to you. Heaven or Hell – It is your life five years from now. God gave you the gift of discernment. He gave you the gift of free will and making your own choices.

Choice

It's a matter of choice. And for every choice you make, you need to know that there is a consequence – good or bad. It can be immediate or in five years. Knowing this, you need to take responsibility for your role. Look at your life – is it where you want it? Can you see your role in how it got to this place? By looking carefully at your choices, you can determine whether to keep or change your behaviors and actions in the future to get your desired outcome.

There are several techniques that will help to reveal to you the potential consequences.

1. Identify the stakeholders in your decisions and how it is going to affect them. Look at your decisions and choices through their eyes. It can be your children, co-workers, relatives i.e. anyone that you are going to have to live or deal with concerning your choices. Who will it help? Who will it hurt? Can it be avoided? Are you prepared to handle that?

2. Run your decisions and choices through your personal sieve, as well as the following character traits of: fairness, trustworthiness, respect, caring, responsibility and community. Will your decision or choice be disrespectful to anyone? Will your decision or choice break any laws or rules? Is it ethical? Are you breaking a promise or lying to anyone?

3. Are you ok if it makes "Front Page News?" A choice that looks good only if no one knows, is not normally a good choice. Character is who we are when no one else is looking. Character is strengthened when you make choices in the mind set of everyone looking.

4. Choice and decision-making are not a science, and sometimes, even with our best efforts, sometimes things go wrong. Always monitor your choices. If they aren't producing the intended results – reassess and make a new choice. You are permitted to change your mind and your choices, you know. It is surprising how many women I deal with who think they must live with a bad decision they made when they were little more than a child. They are socialized to bury their burden and their pain and wear a pasted smile for the rest of their life because of the uneducated decision that they made.

Failure is Important to Success

Listen up Ladies – failure can be your best friend!

Give yourself permission to make some mistakes. As superwomen – perfect wives, perfect mothers, perfect employees, perfect bosses – we just do not allow the hint of falling or failure into our vocabulary, and we die a thousand deaths because of it. Changing your mind or changing your choices is not the end of the world. Life is a daily evolution; a living organism that must move, stretch, fall, fail, feed, rise, grow, propagate etc. It is not a solitary event.

If you feel you have fallen or failed in a particular aspect of your life, pick yourself up, dust yourself off, and say thanks to your God for the opportunity to have experienced the lesson. Then DO learn from it and move on as a better person, with more clarity of vision as to what is right for you and your life. If you don't fall and fail, you remain a child, protected in a comforting cocoon, only able to peek out through the silk strands at life and wish you could participate. Many a child bride dies of old age in the cocoon.

For those of us who are out here rolling in the mud of life occasionally (strong willed people like me have spent a lot of time in the mud), you pick yourself up, smile through the mud on your face, embrace life and say, "Wow, what a ride! I don't want to do that again, but I wouldn't have missed the opportunity to learn what I have learned and be who I am today because of it."

Gratitude

If I were a cat, I'd be on life nine right now. I've grown, changed, and reflected through the agony of divorce, miscarriage, sexual abuse, mental abuse, failure in career, failure in marriage, poverty, abandonment, isolation, inequality, severe health issues, social death, and loss of love. And, basically, I'm a pretty happy person. Insane? No

– I just have learned how to survive and look for the seed of light in the darkest hour.

I owe it to Mrs. Price, my fourth grade school teacher. Every afternoon Mrs. Price would have us lay our heads on our desk and would read books to us. She read many, but the two I remember the most continue to guide my steps today. She taught us great courage by reading about a boy 'Mafatu' and his dog Uri in *"Call it Courage"*. It is the story of a young boy who was son of the king, driven to overcome his fear of the sea that had claimed his mother. The cold indifference he experienced from his tribe forced him to search for his courage, his life. *"Call it Courage"* is written by Armstrong Perry and has been in print for over sixty years.

The second book Mrs. Price read was about survival and finding the best in the most horrible of situations. The book is entitled, *"Jonica's Island"* by Gladys Malvern. It is the story of a poor little girl whose mother was dead and her father was an alcoholic. She learned as a tiny girl not to go to bed without counting her blessings. Every night she would try and try and find something good that had happened to her that day – she would "count her gratitudes." I have done that for nearly 50 years. I have tried to look for the best in all situations, to "count my gratitudes."

It is written that you cannot have flow when you are blocked. "Counting your gratitudes" opens the soul and explodes the blockage on your heart when all seems lost. You can feel the hardness push slowly aside and feel the trickle of life come back to your heart. I know. I have been a stone…unbending, unreachable as I closed off to protect myself from more pain. Sometimes my only gratitude I could find was that I could still breathe…

Today, I am just a short time away from my Ph.D. I want to share Mrs. Price's soft voice as she read the words of life to those tiny children. I want to show Jonica's heart as she found the blessings in each day. I need Mafatu's courage to take a stand for women in the midst of atrocities, rather than live my now comfortable life and ignore the cries of continuing pain because they do not have the answer.

I wonder if Mrs. Price knew, in those sleepy afternoons, that her soft rhythmic words would save a heart, a soul, a life…

When all you can see is up because you can't sink any lower, look for your God's smile and take his hand. Begin the climb. The secret to never being in the hole again – *learn* your lessons with each step you take, and each choice you make. If you don't, you are guaranteed to fall and fail again and again because the behavior, decision-making and choices that you are using are the ones that you know and are familiar with that led you to the pit. Change the patterns. Change the choices. Change the decisions. Change the behavior. Change comes from within!

I have fallen.
I have failed.
I have survived.
I have succeeded.
I have lived!

Notes:

ABOUT THE AUTHOR

Heidi Ciuzio- Santiago RN CLNC

Heidi Ciuzio –Santiago was born in Bronx, New York, and currently resides in Monroe, New York with her four teenage children and two teacup poodles. She has been in the healthcare industry for over twenty five years and has spent most of that time in home care both in the role of field nurse and management.

In 2000 Heidi earned her certification as a Legal Nurse Consultant, and founded her own consulting business. She was featured in CLNC Success Stories from the Vicky Millazo Institute and is currently pursuing her Bachelors/Masters in Public Health.

In her role as mother, Heidi has served as the President of the Parents Auxiliary for the New York Military Academy for four consecutive years, raising thousands of dollars for the student body. She considers her children her greatest achievement.

Heidi joined the corporate arena in 2005 and has since been a leader in sales of cutting- edge wound care, educating hundreds of physicians/nurses and home care management in top wound care techniques.

Heidi Ciuzio-Santiago considers her presentations to be honest, humorous and upbeat which she considers a reflection of her life philosophy.

Contact:
Heidi25@optonline.net

EIGHTEEN

HEALTHY EATING: GETTING FIT

By Heidi Santiago

Healthy eating and getting fit, is there any topic besides money that gets more press or has more time devoted to it? Is there any topic that makes us more uncomfortable than this? Be honest! How many of us have lied to our spouses, friends, and even our doctors, about what we eat, what we weigh, or how much exercise we get? How many of us have bought (or better yet wasted) our money on the next great weight loss pill? Well, let me clue you in on a secret (but don't tell the huge weight loss industry); there is no quick fix, no great weight loss pill, and no overnight sensation. What we do have are healthy food choices combined with an active lifestyle.

What I am going to propose to you is a lifestyle change. You can diet if you choose, but unless you make a lifelong commitment to good health, your efforts will be futile. Here's a statistic to wake you all up: heart disease is the leading cause of death in women, NOT breast cancer. And our diet has a direct correlation to heart health! We do so much for others; the least we can do is take care of ourselves.

I am going to ask you to do a few things for yourself. I am going to ask you to commit to your health. As with any commitment, it is usually done best in steps. Following are the top tips I have found over the years that have helped my patients to make and stick to a healthy eating style.

1. First, make an appointment with your doctor. Get a full physical. Know what your cholesterol and your BMI are. Get an honest opinion on your weight and body fat ratio. In other words, get a starting point.

2. Next, make a commitment, a commitment to yourself. Not necessarily to lose weight, but to commit to a healthy lifestyle. And don't do it for anyone but yourself.

3. Next and most importantly, set a goal!! I recommend setting small, short-term goals. For some, the goal may be to lose weight, others to firm up, or just get their cholesterol within an acceptable range. If it's to lose weight, please be realistic; remember, you didn't gain it overnight and you won't lose it overnight. Again, ask your doctor what you need to realistically lose and in what time frame. If you need something very structured, the only true diet plan I recommend is Weight Watchers. It's not extreme and gives many of us the support we need. Please stay away from fad diets, celebrity diets, and any diet that totally eliminates any major food group. Also, PLEASE stay away from ads that claim miracles, or dramatic weight loss changes without lifestyle or eating habit changes.

Healthy Eating: Getting Fit

To help you set your goal, I have included in this chapter two different height/weight charts. Use either, but as a guide, not an absolute. The first is for women and is based on your frame size.

Height In Feet & Inches	Small Frame	Medium Frame	Large Frame
4'10"	102-111	109-121	118-131
4'11"	103-113	111-123	120-134
5'0"	104-115	113-126	122-137
5'1"	106-118	115-129	125-140
5'2"	108-121	118-132	128-143
5'3"	111-124	121-135	131-147
5'4"	114-127	124-138	134-151
5'5"	117-130	127-141	137-155
5'6"	120-133	130-144	140-159
5'7"	123-136	133-147	143-163
5'8"	126-139	136-150	146-167
5'9"	129-142	139-153	149-170
5'10"	132-145	142-156	152-173
5'11"	135-148	145-159	155-176
6'0"	138-151	148-162	158-179

How do you determine your frame size? It's fairly simple.

1. If you are left-handed, extend your right arm. If you are right-handed, extend your left arm.

2. With your free hand, wrap your thumb and middle finger around your extended wrist. Be sure to wrap it around the SMALLEST section of your wrist - very close to where the hand sticks out.

Small Frame: If your middle finger and thumb overlap, you have a small frame.

Medium Frame: If your middle finger and thumb touch, you have a medium frame.

Large Frame: If your middle finger and thumb do not meet, you have a large frame.

The next is the federal government standard guidelines for adults. Again, remember this is a guideline. In choosing this guide, keep in mind that this is for both men and women, with the higher ranges meant for men. Also, these weights are without clothes or shoes. Something else to consider here is that our weight fluctuates (especially women). So, pick a range of 3 to 5 lbs as your goal weight. Most women can fluctuate up to 5 lbs a day.

Federal Government Suggested Weights for Adults			
Height	Weight		
	19 to 34 years		35 and older
5'0"	97 - 128		108 - 138
5'1"	101 - 132		111 - 143
5'2"	104 - 137		115 - 148

5'3"	107 - 141		119 - 152
5'4"	111 - 146		122 - 157
5'5"	114 - 150		126 - 162
5'6"	118 - 155		130 - 167
5'7"	121 - 160		134 - 172
5'8"	125 - 164		138 - 178
5'9"	129 - 169		142 - 183
5'10"	132 - 174		146 - 188
5'11"	136 - 179		151 - 194
6'0"	140 - 184		155 - 199
6'1"	144 - 189		159 - 205
6'2"	148 - 195		164 - 210
6'3"	152 - 200		168 - 216
6'4"	156 - 205		173 - 222
6'5"	160 - 211		177 - 228
6'6"	164 - 216		182 - 234

Are you still with me? Ok, so now we have seen a doctor, made a commitment, and set a goal. Now, where do we go from here? Choose a meal plan that works for you. Below are websites to help you decide on a healthy start. I want you to notice that every one of these sites has a common thread. They are not extreme; they include a variety of foods with an emphasis on natural foods high in fibers and low in fats. They all also contain helpful tips to eat healthy on a daily basis. If you go looking on-line for healthy eating sites, I recommend you stay with the free sites. I stay away from diets I have to pay for. I am going to list the good sites starting with my favorites:

1. www.americanheart.org Scroll to diet and nutrition.
2. www.4women.gov Type healthy diet into site search engine.
3. www.webmd.com/diet
4. www.eatwell.gov.uk Although a UK site, I found it very helpful with many useful tips.
5. www.deliciousdecisions.org Besides having delicious heart-healthy foods, each recipe has the breakdown of nutrition facts, including serving size, calories and fat content.

Now ladies, don't go anywhere. Healthy eating is only the first step. There's more to good health than what we eat. First, what we need to discuss before we get into exercise are healthy habits. The only one I really want to talk about is smoking. Simply stated, if you do smoke, STOP! There is absolutely no good reason to smoke. And before you say, "Oh, easy for her to say stop", let me tell you I am an ex-smoker. No, I am not getting up on a soapbox, and no, it wasn't easy to quit. I understand the difficulty and willpower it takes. But I implore you, if you do smoke, when you go see your doctor for that check up I talked about, ask about the new medications to help even chain smokers quit. Remember, I said good health is about choices, so choose to LIVE!

Now, here is the fun part. Get up and get moving. If you are sedentary, almost anything you begin doing on a regular basis will help to increase your metabolism. Commit to doing something physical every day. No, you don't need to join a gym (unless you want to). You do, however, need to get up and move. My favorite way to begin what I call my exercise regime is to walk. You see articles on walking in all the women's magazines and on all the fitness web sites because it works. It's cheap, it's easy, and you can vary intensity just by making slight changes. I am going to give you a simple step-by-step guide to walking for health. Before you start though, there is a small investment you need to make, and believe me this is minor compared to what a gym or personal trainer would cost you. You will need a really good pair of walking sneakers, not running shoes. There is a difference. Make sure they fit well and have room to breathe. Next, you will need some clothes appropriate for the weather. I walk in most weather and do dress appropriately. I do not like jeans for exercise. They afford limited flexibility and don't breathe well. Trust me! Invest in some decent walking attire.

So, now we are ready.

1. Decide where you will walk. Avoid busy streets or roads with no shoulder. If your town has a bike path or park, those places are usually ideal. If you are lucky, the route will have the mileage posted somewhere.

2. Pick a time that works best for you. If you are not a morning person, don't start getting up extra early to fit walking into your day. You will just wind up resenting it and quit. But once you pick a time, commit to it. Come hell or high water, get out there and move.

3. Set a goal. I know, it sounds impossible, but goals work! Start small, maybe 10 minutes a day at a quick pace and 5 minutes at a slower pace, for the first week. Then, progressively increase your time by 5 to 10 minute increments weekly. If you don't like the idea of being limited to time, set a distance as your goal. Maybe ½ mile a day for the first week, increasing by ½ mile increments weekly. You need to walk at least 4-5 days a week. I have read in many magazines and articles that 3 days a week is enough, and that might be true, but it is my experience that if exercise is not part of your daily routine, you will not do it.

4. You may need to enlist a buddy. Some of the best times and memories I have are on long brisk walks with my daughter. We motivated each other, and during some rocky teen times it kept our relationship solid. And we didn't let each other off the hook!

Walking is the best exercise I know. If you have been at it for a while and need a challenge, I have some suggestions:

1. Change where you walk. Move to a more challenging course, one with hills. Some parks have fitness trails with workout stations.

2. Increase your pace, a brisk pace for 10 minutes followed by a slower pace for 2 minutes and repeat the pattern. I like to power walk. It's not quite as hard on the joints as running, but has all the benefits.

3. Add weights; carry light to medium hand weights. It makes a difference!

4. Believe it or not, raise those arms. Raising your arms above heart level increases your heart rate. You can alternate raising and lowering your arms throughout your walk.

5. Lastly, walk to music. Studies show that when you walk to music, you tend to work out longer and more vigorously.

Now, walking isn't for everyone. If you have weak knees, bad feet or any multitude of health problems, find something that you can do. If you are a senior citizen, call your local center and see what is available. If it's an issue because you don't want to work out in public, go buy some inexpensive workout videos and exercise/walk at home. (A word of caution with the tapes: always work at your own pace.) Pain does not equal gain. A slight muscle burn is good, pain is not.

Then there are those of us that need structure and a designated workout place. That's fine too. Join a gym, but my suggestion is to shop around for a gym that is right for you. Look for convenient hours, cleanliness, knowledgeable staff, and one that fits your budget. If being in a gym with men intimidates you, look for a women-only workout center. There are women-only workout centers popping up all over America, and they tend to be less expensive. Their only drawback is that hours tend to be limited. See if they will give you a trial period before you commit. Lastly, and probably least expensive is your local YMCA. They generally have good deals for town residents.

OK Ladies, you know what to do. Now go do it! And have fun while you are at it! Just think, the best is yet to come. Good Luck. YOU CAN DO THIS!

ABOUT THE AUTHOR

Ruby M. Ashley, MBA

Ruby Ashley is Chief Executive Officer of Ruby Ashley & Associates. She is a leader in personal and professional development, specializing in the delivery of workshops, seminars, training programs, and assessments. Her workshops and training programs are highly interactive and stimulating with focus on improving employee performance. She firmly believes that as long as individuals are willing to learn, change, and grow, they will always reach high levels of achievement.

Ms. Ashley is an accomplished motivational keynote speaker, facilitator, trainer, and consultant with more than 26 years of experience in the corporate environment. As a Certified Customer Service Trainer, she delivers an outstanding Customer Service Excellence program. Other training program topics include: personal and professional development, women's issues, diversity and multiculturalism, self-esteem, leadership development, strategic planning, road map to retirement, and team building. Teen topics are Save Our Youth, Teen Image, and Leadership.

Ms. Ashley earned Bachelor's and Master's degrees in Business from Brenau University in Gainesville, GA. She is a member of The Professional Woman Network (PWN), is a certified trainer, and member of The PWN International Advisory Board. Ms. Ashley holds memberships in other professional organizations, including the American Business Woman Association, Toastmasters International, Les Brown Speaker's Bureau. She is a youth mentor and an active volunteer in her community.

Ruby Ashley is also a co-author of *Becoming the Professional Woman, Self-Esteem & Empowerment for Women* and *The Young Woman's Guide for Personal Success* in the PWN Library.

Contact
Ruby Ashley & Associates
1735 Chatham Ridge Circle #206
Charlotte, NC 28273
(404) 316-5931
rbyash@aol.com
www.protrain.net

NINETEEN

WHERE DO YOU GO FROM HERE? CHOOSING YOUR FUTURE

By Ruby Ashley

Tell me, what else should I have done?
Doesn't everything die at last, and too soon?
Tell me, what is it you plan to do
with your one wild and precious life?
—Mary Oliver, **A Summer Day**

A View with an Attitude

Mary Oliver makes a good point. We only have one life to live, and it is very precious. Have you thought about what you are doing with yours? Is your life going in the direction you want? If not, what are you going to do to change it? Sometimes life-changing decisions are difficult, but they are most always worthwhile.

Remember that every day is a new day and a chance for you to start over. Think about how you begin each day. Do you jump out of bed every morning looking forward to what life has in store for you, or do you reset the alarm clock because you dread the work you have to do? It's your choice. How you view the world is all about your attitude. If you have a positive attitude, you will find that good things are happening to you. However, when you have a bad attitude, you'll find all kinds of things going wrong in your life. It's a self-fulfilling prophecy. You get what you expect, so if you believe that bad things always happen to you, then you will find that you are right. Life is your glass – either half empty or half full. You decide each an every day where you will go from here and what direction your life will take. Start an inventory of your life. Ask yourself the following questions:

- How do you feel about your life today?

- Are you happy?

- What do you think about how your life is going?

- Are you doing what you always wanted to do?

- What type of moment are you experiencing in your life right now? Are you having a "down" moment, a "pause" moment, a "just waiting" moment, or an, "I need help" moment?

- Are you trying to pick up the pieces and move on because of some kind of tragedy you have experienced?

- Is this where you want to be right now, or do you feel the need to change something?

Self-Analysis

To help you decide if you are going in the right direction with your life, you need to first determine if you like who you are and if you need to make any changes in yourself. The only way to discover how you feel about yourself and your life is to do an in-depth self-analysis.

A great way to do this is to take a look in the mirror and determine if you like what you see. You should take into account your physical attributes such as smooth skin, fine lines, wrinkles, etc. But you should also look at the person you are: friendly, generous, loving, etc. Look in the mirror at two different times. The first time, just look at yourself objectively, letting your thoughts and feelings be whatever they are. Then wait awhile and go back to the mirror, specifically looking at yourself to see if you feel the need to make any changes. Feel free to talk to yourself if you want – just as you would talk to your best friend, because that person in the mirror is someone who you should care a lot about. Be honest. Acknowledge both the good and bad features you see. After looking at yourself in the mirror both times, determine whether you saw anything different the second time than you did the first time. If so, was it because you were willing to communicate your thoughts the second time, rather than just observing them as you did the first time? Be willing to make the necessary changes to become the person you want to be, as this will help you discover the innate inner beauty you have that perhaps isn't being reflected back to you in the mirror at this moment in time. I want you to get to a place that, when you look at yourself in the mirror, you don't see all your faults, flaws, and shortcomings, but rather the beautiful individual you were created to be. So how do you get to that place where you can see your inner beauty?

The Colorful Canvas of Your Life

You create the person you want to be by the decisions you make every day. I want you to imagine that you are an artist and that your life is a blank canvas. Each and every day you are given the opportunity to paint your world any way you want using whatever colors and details you desire. You will choose the colors for your canvas that will represent your day. What you have going on in your life will have a great deal to do with the colors you choose. For me, today I chose green and red as my primary colors. Then I added a splash of yellow. Why did I choose these colors? Because today is Saturday, and I have a lot of things on my "to do" list. I chose the color green to represent "go." I have several projects that I need to go ahead and get started on today. On the other hand, I picked the color red to remind myself that I need to stop doing things that distract me from my primary goals today. Then, I decided to splash a little yellow into the mix in order to caution myself to slow down so that I don't get too stressed, and to make sure I keep myself on track. Through self-actualization, I'm able to visualize myself as the painter standing at the canvass using these three colors while I smile and let my mind and body absorb the beautiful feeling of the end result, a masterpiece of a day where I was able to get my "to do" list accomplished. Only you can choose the colors that would be perfect for your day because different colors mean different things to different people.

For example, I called a friend of mine yesterday and asked her to visualize herself as a painter with a blank canvas to see what colors she would choose for her day, and why. She did not waste any time telling me the colors for her canvas today would be black and red. She chose these colors because she was on her way to a business meeting, and she was wearing a black suit with a red blouse. For her, the black suit represented stylish business attire, while the red blouse made her feel excited, daring, and ready to face any challenge. After relating her colors for the day, I shared my choices of green, red, and yellow with her. Then out of curiosity, I asked her what the color yellow meant to her. She quickly replied, "opportunity." Obviously, there was a stark difference between what the colors red and yellow meant to her, and what they meant to me. Why? Because we are two women with different plans, visions, and goals for the day.

Now it's your turn. Think about your day. What colors would you choose for your canvass today?

_____
_____

Why?

_____
_____
_____

The idea of imagining yourself as an artist, painting your canvas with colors you chose to complement your day, is powerful. The purpose of choosing colors for your day is to make you conscious of the choices you make that will influence what happens in your life. Caution! When your day is filling up with things that seem to be negative, take a step back and analyze what is happening. Determine how much impact your attitude is having on making the situation either worse or better.

Then, try to make positive decisions that take into account what is best for everyone involved.

Since you never know what is going to happen in life, you have to be flexible. Realize that you have the freedom to change the color of your paint at any time during your day. You can also toss out the old drawing and start again, painting whatever you want on your new blank canvas. Just remember not to lend your brush to others who may have a different vision than you. After all, nobody knows better what you want to do with your life than you do. So, if you choose to paint with certain colors, don't let others influence you to let them take over your painting. If you do, you will find that you haven't been able to create what you wanted, but rather you lost your focus and allowed someone else to create something that didn't really reflect the real you. Remember that today this particular moment in time is all we have, so make sure you are living your true colors.

Looking To The Future

When you color your day, you are using your creative mind to bring your vision and goals to life. While you may never have thought about using your imagination to help you solve your problems, this inner resource is always available to you. It allows you to think of creative solutions to even the most difficult problems. When was the last time you had an idea and it worked? Were you surprised that the thought just seemed to come 'out of the blue'? In reality, your idea came from inside of you and is a product of your imagination. And guess what? There's more where that came from! You have so many ideas inside of you that are just waiting to be discovered! All you have to do is to be open to the creative force inside of you. Some might say this is a divine force that is connected to a higher universal power. Whether or not that is true, one thing for sure is that it is unique to each individual.

So tomorrow, when you wake up, visualize your day as a blank canvas, keeping in mind that you, and only you, are the artist creating your world. Think about something you want to do or the things you want to accomplish throughout the day, and give each of them a color. Remember, there are only 24 hours in a day, so plan accordingly (hint: make your to-do list the night before). As you begin to paint your canvas, bring positive thoughts and imagination into each stroke and color. When you are in front of your canvas, though it is imaginary, see yourself slowly and deliberately creating a beautiful day by imagining only the good and positive. You can make your picture as detailed as you want. Use your own special finesse and power, always keeping in mind the end result you want to achieve. Should you find your canvas seems boring and un-imaginative, try using the mirror technique we discussed earlier to examine your day, and to help you visualize the painting you want to create. In the Norman Vincent Peale book, *Expect A Miracle - Make Miracles Happen*, he quotes naturalist John Burroughs who said, *"My own shall come to me."* He means that what we send out mentally and spiritually will return to us. In essence, we become what we are in our thoughts.

Try the following exercise at the end of your day, visualizing yourself as the artist who is making the strokes/decisions for tomorrow.

Describe your plan or goal for tomorrow:

_____

_____

What colors did you choose for painting your canvas?
_____
_____

Why?
_____
_____
_____
_____

Think back to today. Did you have to change you colors/direction at any time during the course of your day?
Why or why not?
_____
_____
_____

Outcome – How do you feel now about the selections of colors you chose for today and tomorrow?
_____
_____
_____

Overcoming Fear

Sometimes we find ourselves being afraid to step out, step up, and try something different.

Life can sometimes be overwhelming and just a bit too much to handle; however, you have to remember that it's your life. You should know better than anyone what's really going on with you, and you should have a plan of action that allows you to do what you can, fix any problems you encounter, and keep moving on. One thing is sure: you cannot place your life on hold or ask it to stop and wait until you are ready.

Hopefully, your future holds many positive days. To make a brighter tomorrow for ourselves, we must start with making a better today. You have the power to make each day the day you want it to be. However, if you don't have a vision or goal, you will lack the direction you need to go in a positive direction. If you go through your day accepting whatever life throws at you rather than planning what you want, you will feel powerless and find your life spiraling out of control. On the other hand, if you decide what you want to do and take the steps you need to take in order to accomplish what you want, you will call on your own internal strength and power to gain control over the circumstances in your life. While it's true that "life happens" (meaning there will be unforeseen circumstances out of your control), you always have the power to decide how you react and what decisions you will make. Some will be as a result of your own doing, while others will be because there is a greater force than you and I that has control over everything and everybody. What I do believe is that once we've established a habit or a routine, we can, at any time, sit down and look at our lives to determine where we are, and to answer the question: Where do I go from here? Once we have the answer, we will be able make the right choices and decisions, for not only today, but also all the future days to come. Remember, when you feel fear, pick up your paintbrush and canvas. Choose a color that will overcome your fear, and help you feel alive and hopeful. Keep that "paint can" in your mind when you come across any obstacles, and visually paint yourself *into a more positive mood. Where do you go from here?* You have the answers, the paintbrush, the colors, and the strength to color your world just as you wish, now and in the future.

> *If You Always Do*
> *What You Have Always Done,*
> *Then You Will Always Get*
> *What You Have Always Got.*
> *If You Want Something*
> *That You Have Never Had,*
> *Then You Need To Do*
> *Something That You Have*
> *Never Done.*
> *If You Always Think The Way*
> *You Have Always Thought,*
> *Then You Will Always Get*
> *What You Have Always Got.*
> —(Author Unknown)

Where do you go from here? Simply put, make a fresh start or a new beginning. A new beginning can only occur when you decide to put an end to the negative things that are happening now in your life so you can get different results. Be **BOLD,** stand up to yourself, and say, "Enough is enough." You have a very important life to live, YOURS.

And you are a beautiful person who is going to bring your own special hues to the rainbow of life, making it a more colorful and vibrant place to be.

Recommended Reading

Yesterday, I Cried **by Iyanla Vanzant**

In Pursuit of Happiness: Knowing What You Want, Getting What You Need **by E. Perry Good**

ABOUT THE AUTHOR

Martha Kirby

Martha Kirby is a passionate believer in helping women and youth to grow spiritually and emotionally. She has received training in ministry, is certified as a consultant on Women's Issues, and is a Certified Life Coach.

Ms. Kirby has been employed in the United States Army Reserve and holds a B.S. in Information System Management.

She is available to present workshops for women and youth on personal empowerment and emotional wellness. Martha Kirby is an advocate of teaching the Word of God so that people can understand the importance of respecting others regardless of race, gender, ethnicity or age.

Contact:
Martha Kirby
P.O. Box 2404
Stockbridge, GA 30281
minkirby@gmail.com
www.protrain.net

TWENTY

SELF-TALK: BECOMING YOUR OWN BEST FRIEND

By Martha Kirby

The best way to become your own best friend (BF) is to ask yourself what it is you look for in a best friend. Then, become that best friend to yourself. I asked some friends of mine a "best friend" question recently, just to get a conversation going amongst us. Here is what some of them had to say.

Know Yourself

One friend said she has had the same best friend since she was six. That says a lot. First, it states she knows how to keep friends by being a friend. It also tells us, this BF is someone she has known a long time, more than half her life. This BF must know all the hidden secrets about her, what makes her laugh, as well as cry. She knows when she is upset. This BF accepts her for all her promises and all her faults. These two women must have shared a lot over the years.

The first thing you must know is yourself. You should examine who you are, what makes you happy, sad, brings you joy, and sets you apart from all the other people in the world. You must know your strengths and your weaknesses. There is nothing wrong with self-examination. No one should be able to tell you anything about yourself you do not already know and recognize.

There is nothing anyone can tell me about myself that I do not already know. There are no surprises in what they say. Sometimes someone will say something about me that may hurt. But rest assured, I already know my issues. Just hearing them out loud may shake me a little.

Be Honest With Yourself

Someone said her best friend is a person you can be honest with. Someone who will be honest with you when you are acting crazy, without hurting your feelings.

It is okay to be honest with yourself about those hidden secrets, no matter how ugly they may be. They are a part of what makes you who you are. If you understand them, then you can continue to grow from them. We are not going to like everything we know about ourselves. But you cannot change what is done.

> *"When you do not live by yesterday, then you start to live for tomorrow."*—Yogi Bhajan

All you can do is learn from your life's lessons. Too often, women will sit and continue to beat up on themselves doing the "would have, could have, should have" game. You cannot go back to yesterday; we can only go forward in life.

I'm always telling friends, life is a learning lesson. There are no failures or errors, just poor choices we have made with the information we had at the time. We need to learn from those choices and not keep making them, or let them hold us back from being what we were intended to be.

Exercise

Take out a piece of paper. Fold it in half. On one side, make a list of all the things you are proud of, and the things you have accomplished. On the other side, make a list of all the things you need to learn from, and all the things you have neglected to complete. This list should include all things unflattering in your life. Now, tear the paper in half. Take the non-flattering list and tear it up. With each tear, verbally release any feelings you may have about them. (i.e. I'm no longer held by my past habits of self-destruction).

Respect Yourself

Another friend said her best friend is someone who respects her and someone she respects. You have to learn to respect yourself. We all have done some things that caused other people to judge us. We have behaved in unkind ways, or taken advantage of other's kindness. Or, we have allowed others to be disrespectful of us. We need to learn to stand tall and be proud of ourselves.

To maintain self-respect, I set goals along my journey. I keep myself motivated and encouraged to the end. As I meet each milestone, I encourage myself in various ways. I like to shop, so I may buy myself something new as a celebration of self!

Exercise: On a piece of paper write down all the reasons you respect yourself. This is a good motivating and encouraging tool for when you have your pity party, which you will learn about in the next section.

Encourage Yourself

Another friend said her best friend is there to pick her up. She knows when something is going wrong in her life, and she encourages her through the rough times. We need to know how to encourage ourselves, but also realize that it is okay to have a pity party every now and then. Someone once told me to buy a kitchen timer and set it for 15 minutes. I had a pity party like no other! However, when that timer went off, the party was over. Well, I have added one more thing to that. While I am having my pity party, I am thinking of a plan to resolve the issue I am having. So, the party is not in vain. When the timer goes off, I come out fighting as if my life depended on it. I encourage myself and have a new way of thinking.

I have a friend who is always beating up on herself and putting herself down. I asked her one day why she did this, and told her that she needed to start building herself up. I also told her something I learned a long time ago. With all the other people in the world talking about her, she needs to become her own best friend and speak encouraging thoughts. Each of has the power to become our own encourager, rather than our own worst enemy.

Exercise
Think of some ways you can motivate and encourage yourself.
_____
_____
_____
_____

Adjust Fire

Someone said best friends are not perfect. And neither are we. We need to stop treating ourselves as the "enemy" and adjust our fire. We have all made unwise choices in our lifetimes. We need to stop firing artillery at ourselves. This reminds me of when I was in the military on the firing range. When I first went in, I hated firing a weapon. I couldn't hit a tree if it was ten yards in front of me. I would be out on that range all day in the heat (I do not like to perspire!) trying to hit the target. Then on one of our trips to the range, I learned how to adjust my fire. Now, when I go out on the range, I only have to adjust one time and I am off the line and back in the shade.

That is what we need to do in life. Learn to adjust our fire. When we make unwise choices, we need to adjust whatever it is to get it right. We need to stop "firing at ourselves" and constantly berating ourselves for past mistakes. We must accept our imperfections and attempt to turn them into strengths. We must remove ourselves from our own personal firing line. We are not our own worst enemy.

My best friend and I like to spend a lot of time together. We examine our relationships. We know each other better than any one else could. Therefore, we are extremely honest with one another. We respect each other like no one else can. And when need be, we adjust fire in our life challenges. We treat ourselves to a monthly pedicure. We go out to eat together. It is safe to say we are not afraid be alone or go out by ourselves. You see, **my best friend is ME**. I never disappoint myself because I know I am not perfect and I understand myself. I accept myself for who I am.

May you learn to become your own best friend by self-encouragement, respect and honesty.

Notes:

ABOUT THE AUTHOR

JANE DENNER

Jane Denner is the principal of **Inner-States, LLC** which is dedicated to the evolution of the whole person –mind, body, and spirit- substituting patterns of success for those of past failures. Emphasis is placed on nutrition and emotional awareness. Ms. Denner is a Certified Professional Consultant and Holistic Health Counselor with over thirty years of experience in the field of natural healing. She is an active member of the Professional Woman Network and serves on its International Advisory Board.

Ms. Denner uses practical exercises to demonstrate that which we hold in our minds can either hold us back or move us forward. Jane provides seminars and coaching to support and guide individuals over the obstacles they encounter on their paths. **Inner-States, LLC** programs help individuals navigate while focusing on nutrition, self esteem and building healthy relationships. Private one-on-one as well as small group coaching sessions, workshops and seminars for all individuals of any age are available. She is passionate about healing through physical and emotional self awareness and strongly believes in being her own example. Jane Denner is a native of Canada and resides in Massachusetts with her family.

Contact:
Inner–States LLC
P O Box 474
Concord, MA 01742
[617] 605 6205
Jane777comcast.net
www.protrain.net

TWENTY-ONE

YOUR MIRROR REFLECTION: WHAT ARE YOU ATTRACTING?

By Jane Denner

"A man's true wealth is the good he/she does in the world. Beauty is eternity gazing at itself in a mirror. But you are eternity and you are the mirror." —Kahlil Gibran

The first time I can remember catching a glimpse of my reflection in the mirror, I was a young girl jumping on my parents' bed with unfettered exuberance. I stopped jumping and gazed with amazement at my body, wondering who was having so much fun inside this newly discovered form. It was a curious moment, the mystery of which I did not fully understand until many years later. What I did understand then however, at that magical moment, was that I totally approved of myself and was thrilled to be alive. Now years later, after a lifetime of being conditioned to feel imperfect by the limited perceptions of others, I think back to that faraway moment and unabashedly yearn for the nearly forgotten feelings of pure joy and acceptance, and seek to understand how to reintroduce them into others lives.

Loving ourselves throughout life is a birthright; it has taken me years of suffering to return to this basic truth. Joy is the natural state of our being. We see this relaxed acceptance in all of nature, and if humans are the crown of creation, then surely we should be overflowing with contentment and joy.

The bad news is that most of us are not all that happy. We have internalized the lies fed to us, and accepted the myth of our imperfection as fact. Fear, rather than joy, drives us. Our perceived inadequacies and imperfections as reflected in the external world haunt us. The good news, however, is that we do not have to choose fear over joy, self-destruction and fragmentation over an integrated, centered self – we have the power to choose and control our physical, emotional and spiritual destinies – the true essence of freedom.

So, let's start the self-excavation from our own personal memories. It is in the facing of old emotional pain as it arises in the present that healing and transformation can begin.

- Can you remember a time before your heart was broken? When was the first time you looked at your form in the mirror and wondered who you were?

_____
_____

- What were your emotions?

_____

_____

- Without dragging out the events that caused you pain, because every one has their own personal story, when did you first start feeling ashamed of your body and who you were?

_____

_____

The different experiences in your life are a reflection of your consciousness, and provide an opportunity to re-evaluate and expand yourself. Becoming self-aware is how you get to know your authentic self, and can then deal with what you want to change in your character as you line yourself up with your essence.

Energy

> *The more you lose yourself in something bigger than yourself, the more energy you will have."* —Norman Vincent Peale

Everything around us, seen and unseen, is energy. It comes in all forms and cannot be created or destroyed, but only can be transformed into another form of energy. If you allowed yourself the emotional freedom to answer the last questions thoroughly, you will have noticed physical sensations occurring in different parts of your body, most probably in the form of discomfort. The uncomfortable sensations may have been experienced in your stomach, heart, solar plexus, or throat areas as they became constricted by regained memories of painful experiences. What you felt was congested, stuck energy.

Let's take a look at the seven basic energy "hubs" located in our body [also known as chakras]. They generate varied physical experiences as energy flows through them, from the base of the torso, up the spine, through the crown of the head. [See Chart.]

The Seven Basic Energy Hubs

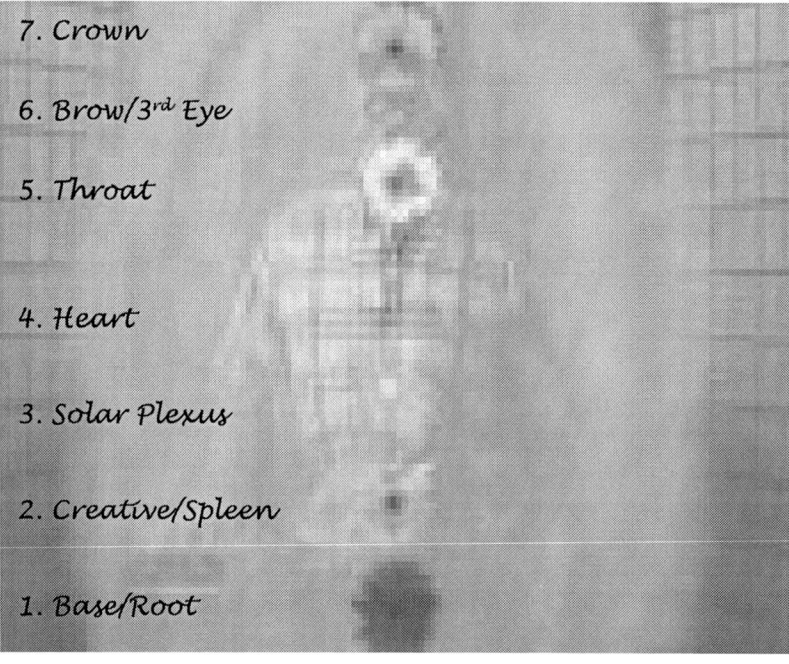

7. Crown

6. Brow/3rd Eye

5. Throat

4. Heart

3. Solar Plexus

2. Creative/Spleen

1. Base/Root

Aura Photo with Chakra Activity
Kirlian photo of a person showing Aura and the 7 Main Chakras 2007 www.auraphoto.com.
Photo used with kind permission from Guy Coggins of Aura Imaging, respected leaders in Kirlian photography.

Becoming Aware of Your Energy

Thoughts produce emotions, which in turn affect the quality of the energy flowing through our energy "hubs". If, for instance, you experienced emotional pain when you wrote down your experiences in the last exercise, the energy passing through your body was congested. Congested energy causes physical pain because it does not flow through the body freely. The hubs or chakras are similar to processing centers wherein the quality of energy is registered. Thoughts /emotions sourced in love will cause the physical body to experience a relaxed, light-hearted feeling, while those derived from fear often produce physical pain and discomfort. The state of our energy hubs is a virtual "snapshot" of where we need to be healed.

For example, if one has long been frightened to speak in public because of a terrifying past public experience, then whenever they are frightened and become emotionally upset, the fear-based generated energy locates itself in the fifth energy hub, the throat chakra. Thus, the proverbial sensation of a tightened throat, "choking up", is the physical sensation which they experience. Naturally, then, to avoid this fearful sensation, these people tend to avoid speaking in public. However, the better course of action would be to control such a conditioned response by pausing and becoming fully present, thus essentially embracing the moment of pain, assuming the role of observer, and becoming the facilitator to allow it to be existentially watched, accepted, and processed with compassion. By objectifying the pain outside of oneself, the "me" then becomes the observer / facilitator and neutralizes the pain by no longer feeding or empowering the fear, the true beginning of the healing process.

On the other hand, if the emotions that pass through you are pleasant and joyful, the energy produced is based in peace and love, and a warm, relaxed sensation, rather than pain, is produced by the free-flow of energy through the hubs. This is the experience of body awareness. When we feel anything other than relaxed, free-flowing energy, our attention is required to assist in the energy transformation and rebirth. To maintain this free-flow requires vigilance against insidious, old thought patterns of fear and uncertainty.

When we train ourselves to look inward and pause, take note of our emotions as they rise up and pass through us, we can see that the emotions and the energy hubs are **informational.** Emotions are the soul's way of conversing with us. Tuning in is a matter of expanding our limited perceptions through turning our attention inward and learning a new language called **body awareness.**

Think of your awareness and free-will as the trigger that can transform congested, fear-based energy into free-flowing love-based energy, obviously preferable as it is painless and we feel happier, freer and returned to our natural state of being. When we choose to listen, learn, and change that which is painful by facing it in the moment, challenging it as it arises with total acceptance, compassion and courage, and choosing not to identify with the pain as "me" the victim, but rather as "I" the essence and witness, we transform ourselves.

In transforming emotional "fear", our complete, present, uncensored attention is required **without thought**. We are focused in the "now" without attachment to the outcome, in complete acceptance of what is taking place in the body, with compassion actively assisting our transformation into something more evolved. We align ourselves with something greater than our "me" persona. The soul speaks to us clearly, if we will but listen. When we become fluent in the language of the soul, we understand that fear is painful and love is peace.

Thus, as we facilitate the rebirthing of our emotions through the filters of love and compassion, we change and expand our own sensory perception and intuition, and become aligned with a greater collective consciousness. We emerge from our limited perception of ourselves through our finite thought, and merge into the sum of the infinite whole. This practice of "emotional awareness" has the power to transform your personal energy. One, in fact, could regard our physical form as an energy transformer for the soul's evolution, only requiring your full attention to reach its fruition.

If focused in the present moment, bearing witness to painful emotion as it arises, you must not be in "**thinking mode**", but rather in "**witness mode**" – relaxed and fully focused, paying attention to your inner vision from the deepest part of the peace that you can find within yourself.

- Experiment with this technique and write down what feelings you discover at the core of your self, beyond your fears.

_____
_____

If you are feeling stuck in your life, (remember, everything is just energy) and you desire change, you need to start paying attention to your inner body signals, utilizing the power of your "will" and changing the choices you make.

"Don't hold to anger, hurt or pain. They steal your energy and keep you from love." —Anonymous

Conscientious Choice

When you choose responsibly for the evolution of your spirit, your energy recharges, expands and soars. It is like fanning a fire with lighter air to kindle, rather than to suffocate, your core fire. It is suffocating your spirit with heavy thoughts that ultimately produces painful emotions and poor choices. We tend to identify with our thoughts, and think that our thoughts are who we are. It is the mental myth that you have painstakingly constructed over the years to create the "perfectly acceptable you" which ultimately drains your energy and essence, consigning you to being the external world's conception of you, rather than your truest self. Only when we align our character with our essence, which is infinitely more than the sum total of our finite thoughts, do we start the journey of recovery and rebirth. Your choice of love over pain is not denial. Quite the contrary, it is having the courage to face your deepest fears and challenges, to transform the painful energy into the possibility of greater awareness.

What energy are you feeding? Your inner essence / soul or your character / personality?

<u>Essence</u> or	<u>Character</u>	<u>Essence</u> or	<u>Character</u>
Love	Hate	Victor	Victim
Joy / Ease	Anger	Forgiving	Resentment
Responsibility	Blame	Acceptance	Rejection
Encouraging	Hopeless	Freedom	Controlling
Enthusiastic	Apathetic	Harmony	Disagreement
Sharing	Defensive	Embraces	Avoids

Courage	Fear	Collaborates	Scheming
Intimacy	Power Struggle	Intuitive	Limited Perception
Growing	Stagnant	Integrity	Dishonesty
Compassion	Judgment	Appreciation	Jealousy
Trust	Suspicion	Self-Love	Self-Doubt
Bravery	Insecurity	Do Your Best	Denial

What choices will you make in order to transform your energy so that your character is in alliance with your true essence?

In order to grow and change, we have to gain control over our emotions, rather than the converse. As our emotions are a product of our thoughts, we must become aware of our thoughts, and thus aware of the emotions being produced. Look in your own mirror. How are you behaving? How do you relate to the rest of the world, and how does the world relate to you? Gaining control is a matter of awareness, courage, choice, intentions and discipline.

> *"Watch your thoughts, for they become words.*
> *Watch your words, for they become actions.*
> *Watch your actions, for they become habits.*
> *Watch your habits, for they become character.*
> *Watch your character, for it becomes your destiny."* —Frank Outlaw

Most of us live 24/7 in our own private world of thought. Our thoughts consist of either memories of the past or dreams of the future – we rarely live in the present. Our thought process actually slows down and become "still" when we are fully engaged in the moment, where our authentic life actually occurs. When we are not conscious of the present, our thoughts are as wild horses, running untamed with no real direction, out of control. It is in the moment of conscious presence that control is regained and healing takes place. When we no longer feed our emotions with chaotic thought, we become able to live in the stillness and the peace of the moment.

When you hold your negative emotions with love and compassion in the present moment, you will find and experience your authentic self, and the promise of a positive, proactive rather than a negative, reactive, awareness.

Intention

Intention is motivation in action. If your dream is to change something in your character, you must have clear intentions about what you want to change. Bring awareness by watching your behavior and frequently asking yourself – what was the real intention behind my actions? Was it to boost my image, seek exterior power by having control over others in order to make myself feel stronger, or was my intention to know and develop my genuine inner self? Set your intentions clearly, so that you become aware of old patterns in your personality that need to be looked at and changed. This is creating genuine power. Understand what energy is running you; is it **fear** or **love?**

Experiment with your intentions. What are three new intentions that you would like to set for yourself?

1. _____
2. _____

3. _____

- Are your intentions set for superficial [external] or genuine, [internal] purposes?

_____

- Is the emotion that is driving your intention fear or love based?

_____

Do not be too hard on yourself when you discover that much of what you desire is fear-based. We have been trained to react in fear by our families and the collective consciousness of society. This consciousness is based in survival perception, and has been predominate in our consciousness for thousands of years. Once you discover that fear has been at the core of your actions, then new choices can be made to genuinely empower yourself. Learning how to genuinely empower is an opportunity to broaden your perceptions, awaken your intuitions, and discover your real purpose. Liberating yourself from your fears is the greatest gift you can give to your self. We can only be free when we live in appreciation of the present moment.

Getting to know You: 101

1. Do I have to have the last word in a discrepancy? YES / NO
2. Do I have numerous arguments? YES / NO
3. Do I take others remarks and behaviors personally? YES / NO

4. Do I feel jealous when someone else gets more attention than I do? YES / NO

5. Do I always have to be the winner in each situation? YES / NO

6. Do I interrupt when others are talking? YES / NO

7. Do I think about what I am going to say rather than giving my full attention and really listing when someone else is talking? YES / NO

If you answered **yes** to any of these questions, you are pursuing external control over your environment and feeding your fears. You are being driven by your primitive fear-based emotion for survival, rather than focusing on the genuine power of your inner essence. Always ask yourself what your intentions are when you catch yourself doing any of the above. Stop, feel the emotion that is rising up inside of you, acknowledge its presence, hold the painful emotions with compassion and respect – choose differently. This is the recipe for inner change to take place; you are at the control panel and you have to initiate the change.

What Are You Attracting?

What you are attracting in life depends on what you are creating. "Like attracts like." If you do not like what you have in your life, and expect that at some future date things randomly will change, you are wrong! The only path to change is a disciplined, determined choice to consciously effectuate it!

- Think about the other people in your life that you interact with and create a list of who you are attracting. Finish the list and write down the characteristics the people around you have. **For example, are they.......**

Angry	...or...	Serene
Revengeful	...or...	Accepting
Gossipy	...or...	Secure

PERSON IN MY LIFE	CHARACTERISTICS

If difficult people continue to inhabit your inner circle, you will find traces of the same dislikable characteristics in yourself that need changing. As you become compassionate with yourself and forgive your own perceived shortcomings, so will you become compassionate with others. You will stop feeding your thoughts with desire, anger, pain or jealously and start paying attention to the emotions you need to heal in your own life. **Remember, it is never really about somebody else, it's always about you.**

If your desire is to become genuine and be surrounded by more conscious people, what fear-based characteristics do you need to work on and change?

- _____
- _____

Your spirit wants to experience sharing and agreement with others, and awareness of itself. If you feel discord in your life, it is because you have not yet aligned your behavior/character with your authentic inner essence. The longest distance is often the journey taken from a person's head to his heart. Take the inward journey; it is the greatest expedition you will ever make. **Be the example**. This is how we change the world, one person at a time, one insight at a time.

Review of Steps for Creating Genuine Consciousness

1. **Find awareness** of your emotions and how they affect you physically in the energy hubs of your body.

2. **Hold, without thought,** your inner vision of peace and compassion the painful emotions, so that the congested energy might move freely and transform into the love that you are consciously bathing it in.

3. **Choose** how the energy that passes through you will be experienced by you. Will you identify with the fear and grow more suffering, or choose to bathe the painful emotions in compassion, heal them, and feel free?

4. **Intention** is being clear on what is driving your actions. Are your intentions fear- based external control seeking, or love-based, internal, genuine power?

5. **Attraction** – "Like attracts like." What are you attracting? Not sure where you are at in your own personal evolution? Look around you, and then look inside yourself. Remember, your purpose is to enjoy your life.

Do not simply read the handwriting on the wall of your soul. Be the one who writes it! Forgive thyself. Love thyself. **Know thyself.**

ABOUT THE AUTHOR

Mardi Allen

Mardi Allen, a Certified Life Coach and Women's Wellness Expert, is passionate about motivating and coaching women to consistently achieve life-changing results and to reach their full potential. She inspires others to create a healthy lifestyle by embracing their own power and breaking self-imposed limitations.

As the Founder and President of Allen Coaching & Training (ACT), specializing in personal and professional development, Mardi's goal is to empower others to enhance their own excellence through workshops, seminars, corporate training, and one-on-one coaching.

As a business leader, entrepreneur, trainer, consultant, and professional life coach, Mardi has been involved in the training and development of thousands of employees. She has been instrumental in implementing programs in self-esteem, stress management, customer service, professional image, and time management for numerous companies. Some of her most popular seminars are Change Your Thinking, Change Your Life, Confidence: Finding the Power Within, and Health and Emotional Wellness.

As a Life Coach specializing in Women's Wellness and Weight Management, Mardi has coached and motivated hundreds of women to attain their ideal weight and taught them the tools to maintain healthy lifestyles. Mardi will be publishing her own book about overcoming weight issues by changing one's mindset.

Mardi is a Certified Trainer with the Professional Woman's Network and is also co-author of *Overcoming the Superwoman Syndrome* and *Women's Journey to Wellness: Mind Body & Spirit*. She is a frequent guest on *The Word FM* radio station in Dallas, Texas, discussing the importance of making the right choices for a healthy lifestyle.

Mardi's life journey and personal path have been instrumental in helping others to be the best that they can be. Her extensive background in human behavior, management, and coaching is the foundation for her success.

Contact:
Mardi Allen
Allen Coaching & Training (ACT)
(214) 649-1320
www.coachmardi.net
mardi@coachmardi.net

TWENTY-TWO

WOMEN VS. WOMEN: HOW TO OVERCOME GOSSIP & SABOTAGE

By Mardi Allen

"So live that you would not be ashamed to sell the family parrot to the town gossip." —Will Rogers

In doing research for this book, I interviewed many women, and every one had at least one story of sabotage or gossip instigated by another woman. Additionally, it is reported that on-the-job sabotage costs American businesses billions of dollars each year.

Sabotage

Why do women sabotage and gossip about other women? We know it happens in politics, business, in our personal lives, and even with family and friends. Why do some women feel like they have to sabotage someone else in order to feel successful or fulfilled themselves?

How we feel about ourselves determines how we live our lives. Self-esteem is the key to how we behave, and how we treat others. If we believe in ourselves, recognize our own capabilities, empower our confidence, and determine that we can handle anything, then there is no need to gossip or sabotage anyone. Often times, when someone feels a need to sabotage, it is a great example of someone with low self-esteem and lacking confidence.

Overcoming Sabotage

The best way to overcome sabotage is to first not contribute to it. It has to start with each and every woman committing to live authentically, and to set a higher standard for herself and those she associates with. Take the high road and stay true to your convictions. Be the best you can be. Set your standards high and live a life of integrity and grace.

If someone has transgressed against you, revenge is not the answer. You do not want to lower yourself to her level with acts of anger, revenge, and hate. You can always choose to believe in yourself, and to get through challenges with grace and integrity. Chose to be the best you can be. Doing well is the best revenge.

Two Levels of Energy

There are two levels of energy: positive and negative. When we have positive energy, it strengthens us; conversely, when we have negative energy, it weakens us. When we judge and hold on to resentment and hate, it is like drinking poison and expecting the other person to die.

There is Enough for Everyone

Women often sabotage other women because they believe that "if they succeed, it takes away from me." Some women are under the impression that there is not enough to go around. The universe is vast and unlimited, and there is enough for everyone. Women must believe in themselves and focus on their own abilities and strength. It always comes back to how we feel about ourselves, and if we chose to focus or positive or negative energy.

Build the Tallest Building

I recently heard a great analogy about having the tallest building. In order to have the tallest building, you do not have to tear down someone else's building in order to make yours the tallest. You can just work on yours; build it up to be the tallest. Do not worry about what everyone else is doing, just work on being the best you can be without tearing anyone else down. When you believe in yourself, you do not have to tear others down to be successful.

Gossip

People gossip because they feel powerless. Most of the time, we gossip about people because they have done something to us, or we have perceived that they have done something and we do not feel we can go directly to them to discuss the matter. At that time we feel powerless, and in our powerlessness, we lash out and deceptively attack, instead of confronting them. We gossip about them behind their backs, instead of confronting them directly.

Almost all of us can come up with a situation in which someone has offended us or done something to upset us, and rather than confronting that person, we went behind their back and started gossiping.

Most companies have that one person who is the company gossip, the person who is stuck in a situation or job where they feel powerless and become paralyzed, unable to move forward or advance. These people can be capable and talented; however, they may suffer from low self-esteem and lack confidence. If that is the case, that can prevent them from moving forward and creating the life they desire.

When people feel powerless, the result can manifest gossip and lack of loyalty to anyone. These are not bad people; they simply feel powerless, and as a result, make poor choices. Anytime they feel someone had wronged them – real or perceived – they became the victim and create huge stories in their minds about how they have been wronged. With that, they become extremely passive-aggressive, and begin gossiping extensively about the person who wronged them. They essentially create this bundle of anger, frustration, hurt, and pity for themselves. Then, rather than directing it at the person who wronged them in a healthy positive way, they unloaded it on anyone who will listen.

Negative Energy Destroys Your Power

Energy cannot be destroyed; it has to come from somewhere, even negative energy. Oftentimes, these people do not have the self-esteem or the tools to direct it where it needs to go, so they compulsively gossip. Not only are they living in a state of hurt, anger, and frustration;

they are living in constant negative energy. Since negative energy is weakening, it is very difficult for creative juices to flow, and to attract positive things into the lives of those filled with this energy.

Most people are under the impression that they will feel better once they unload the negative energy by gossiping about other people. This could not be further from the truth. Gossiping and creating negative energy actually diminishes your power, and it creates bad karma. Remember always, what we put out is what we get back. There is no avoiding that.

"Revenge is like a boomerang. Although for a time it flies in the direction in which it is hurled, it takes a sudden curve and returns, hitting your own head with the heaviest blow of all."—Author Unknown

Revenge is often a motive for gossip. By gossiping, we seem to feel better about ourselves. But in reality, it is like taking that poison and expecting the other person to die. Becoming empowered is an internal job. We can never become empowered through external means. To become empowered, you must practice integrity and self-discipline. In other words, you have to exercise control over your thoughts and your tongue.

Overcoming Gossip

The road to recovery for people who gossip involves, among other things, increasing self-esteem. The best way to do that is to live authentically and tell the truth, holding ourselves accountable to a higher standard. We increase self-esteem by letting go of our victimhood, taking charge of our lives in a positive way, being assertive, and confronting challenges. Start confronting each situation as it comes, instead of immediately turning to gossip and creating negative energy. Here are the steps to take when you feel upset at a situation or someone.

1. Make a commitment to yourself that you are going to change this behavior and hold yourself accountable.

2. When an upsetting situation arises, stop and take at least an hour to cool down and gain perspective. Do not immediately react; that's the worst thing you can do. Never act on anything until you have had time to center yourself. Often, that requires meditation. Center yourself by doing a breathing exercise and clearing your mind.

3. Release any anger and fear about the situation. It is never a good idea to confront anyone when you are frustrated or angry. Try to give people the benefit of the doubt until you have time to discuss a given situation.

4. Plan out what you want to say. If you think it will help, call someone who can be objective – a friend or your life coach – who can help you sort through what has happened.

5. Write down how you feel, and why you want to confront the person. Stick with "I" statements; stay away from "you" statements. Be honest and direct. Avoid accusations and judgments.

6. Practice what you are going to say. Practice until you feel comfortable.

7. Affirm yourself. You are powerful and you are assertive. You can do this.

8. Contact the person and have the discussion. Be open during the conversation.

Many times things are not as they appear, and a simple conversation can quickly clear up misunderstandings. If that is not the case, express what you need to go forward and offer a solution.

Once you start confronting situations as they arise, there is no longer a need to gossip. As the behavior begins to change, you start to recognize that when you are upset and angry, it is often due to your own insecurities. Conscious of this, you will realize that often times you do not have to confront someone about a particular situation because much of it had been "manufactured" in your own head. As you become more empowered, you will stop manufacturing and creating situations.

When there is a true need to confront someone and to stick up for yourself, you will do it. Every time you hold yourself to that higher standard and confront the situation, you become stronger and more empowered. You will create positive energy for yourself and your fellow workers. Your attitude will change, and you will no longer be the victim; you will be in control of your behavior and in charge of your life.

Conversely, if you find yourself the target of gossip, confront the situation directly. Too often when we feel we are the target of gossip, instead of confronting it, we resort to gossiping ourselves, thus perpetuating the negative behavior. Hold yourself to a higher standard. Immediately confront the person who has targeted you with gossip. Do not lower yourself to her level. Take the high road. Let her know you are coming to her directly and would like her to do the same.

Criticizing

How many of us have been told by our mothers, "If you can't say something nice, don't say anything at all?" Now, how many of us abide by that rule? When was the last time you said something unkind about someone or voiced an unfair judgment? Think about that and be honest with yourself.

The reason we criticize and judge others is because we do not feel good about ourselves. Have you ever seen a really happy confident person making other people sad, or saying mean things about someone else? No, if we are happy and feel good about ourselves, we do not feel a need to judge and say unkind things about other people. It is always easier to judge and reflect on others, rather to take a look at ourselves. It takes a strong sense of self to have the courage to be nonjudgmental. Once again, we all are accountable for the energy we create and release into the world. Remember, violence begets violence – even violent words.

Overcome Being Critical

Exercise
When you feel an urge to criticize or judge anyone, stop and think about it. Then, write down your answers to the following questions.
Why do I feel the need to say bad things about this person?
_____
_____

What am I feeling and why do I feel a need to behave this way right now?
_____
_____

Once you are aware of what you are doing, once you recognize your intentions, you can change your habits. Anytime you feel a need to criticize someone else, first affirm yourself, and then say something nice about that person. Start complimenting others and always do it honestly.

Small people talk about other people. Stop talking about other people and start contributing to the planet with positive powerful conversations. If someone tries to gossip with you, you can change the subject, walk away, or confront it directly and state, "I am not comfortable talking about people."

"The Tongue Has the Power of Life and Death. —Old Proverb

If someone is being critical of you or making false accusations, the best way to handle it is to let it go. The gossip usually comes from jealously, competitiveness, and/or insecurity. Do no take it personally, and do not get defensive or focus on it. Do not let them steal your joy and inner peace. Do not worry about pleasing everyone; you just cannot do that. Run your own race and be the best you can be.

Did you ever notice when someone cuts you off in traffic you get upset? You get so angry, and the entire way home you stew about it. You just cannot let it go. You call your friends and tell them the story. You get home, still upset about the situation, and your bad mood affects your family. Finally, you go to bed still upset about it, and it happened at three o'clock that afternoon! Do not let anyone else ever determine your mood. That person, if he was even aware that he wronged you, probably never gave the situation a second thought. Life is short; do not let anyone take your peace. So, if someone is being critical of you, just let it go.

Did you ever notice when someone cuts you off in traffic you get upset? You get so angry, and the entire way home you stew about it. You just cannot let it go. You call your friends and tell them the story. You get home, still upset about the situation, and your bad mood affects your family. Finally, you go to bed still upset about it, and it happened at three o'clock that afternoon! Do not let anyone else ever determine your mood. That person, if they were even aware that he wronged you, probably never gave the situation a second thought. Life is short; do not let anyone take your peace. So, if someone is being critical of you, just let it go.

Women Supporting Women

We are women and we are strong. It takes courage and self-discipline to stop the cycle of sabotage and gossip. It takes courage to look inside, to do your own work, and to increase your own self-esteem and self-confidence. But we are up to the task. The behavior we have today will create our environment for tomorrow, and will affect the women of future generations. Let's take a stand to have the courage to support each other, and to keep our eye on the truth. Let's be part of the solution and not part of the problem. We can help heal the planet with positive energy. It starts with us. Be courageous!

Notes:

ABOUT THE AUTHOR

Hannah Crutcher

Hannah Crutcher, President and CEO of Hannah Crutcher & Associates, is an educator with over twenty years of experience in higher education. Most of that experience is in career counseling and job placement at six colleges and universities. Her passion for eduction extends to K-12 students as well; she has served as a Brownie Girl Scout troop leader, and president, treasurer, and secretary in the Parent/Teachers Association. Hannah is also a member of the Professional Women's Network International Advisory Board.

Ms. Crutcher received a Bachelor's degree in Speech Education with a minor in drama; she loves live theater and has appeared in such classics as *The Amen Corner*, *The Women*, and *The Merry Widow*. She has a Master's degree in Management and is a certified seminar trainer with particular interest in leadership skills, sales, and customer service.

She and her husband Melvin have been married for thirty years and have two adult children.

Contact:
Hannah Crutcher & Associates
1605 Germantown Parkway
Suite 111-216
Cordova, Tennessee 38016
(901) 604-1700
(901) 753-3988 (Fax)
crutcherf@bellsouth.net
www.protrain.net

TWENTY-THREE

GETTING WELL: HANDLING OUR EMOTIONS

By Hannah Crutcher

Have you ever felt pain and disappointment because someone you loved and trusted betrayed you? No doubt there were many emotions you experienced, including disappointment, disbelief, anger and maybe sorrow. The pain cuts very deep; you can't let it go. No! You *won't* let go. As miserable as we are sometimes, we refuse to let go of the feelings that are keeping us locked in a painful time warp. But if you stop and think, you really are the one in control.

Exercise

Ask yourself the following questions:

1. How did I get here? Make a list of people who upset you and put you onto an emotional roller coaster:

- _____
- _____
- _____

2. Why am I letting someone else control my emotions, therefore my life? Make a detailed list of the *ways* these individuals are upsetting you and controlling your emotions:

- _____
- _____
- _____

3. How do I regain control of my emotions? List the steps you can take to stop the roller coaster ride with the persons listed:

- _____
- _____
- _____

4. Who can I turn to for emotional support? List close friends, clergy or a counselor with whom you might discuss your problems:

- _____
- _____
- _____

5. What is holding me back from letting go of the need to hold on to poisonous or controlling relationships?

- _____
- _____
- _____

Letting Go and Moving On

Once you resolve to let go, stay focused and determined to make it happen. Do not focus on the "what if's." Instead, focus on what is in store for you after you move on from emotionally abusive or controlling relationships. Think about the newfound confidence when *you give yourself permission* to be strong enough to move on.

Do not forget, you are in control. Decide how much time you are going to spend pondering an issue – whether it is 15 or 30 minutes, an hour or a day. When that time is up, then let it go. If you start to think about it again, remind yourself that it is history and you have decided to move on. This is no small feat you are undertaking – so recognize its importance and reward yourself for taking this step.

Exercise
1. List every fun and exciting thing you can think of that can help you move on. (How will your life improve without this emotionally controlling person in your life?)

- _____
- _____
- _____

Stop Keeping Score

How many times have you ended up hurt, disappointed and angry, and you want to immediately start placing the blame on someone else? Have you held bitterness within your heart?

Exercise
Who have you not forgiven? What happened?
I have not forgiven the following people:

- _____
- _____
- _____

This is what I would gain from forgiving them:

- _____
- _____
- _____

To release the pain, consider:

1. You are the one who will carry the emotional "ball and chain" of unforgiveness.
2. Don't try to get even. No one will be the winner.
3. Consider why the other person hurt, betrayed, or lied to you.
4. Consider whether you wish to keep this person in your life. If they are poisonous, let them go.
5. Start a new emotionally healthy life without holding bitterness and anger in your heart.
6. If you were at fault in a situation, learn from your mistake and grow.

Exercise

1. List everything that happened with a particular incident in which you find yourself at fault. **The incident:**

_____

What I did that was at fault:

- _____
- _____
- _____

How I could have handled the situation differently:

- _____
- _____
- _____

2. Actually re-live the experiences, but say what you believe are the right words now. Envision yourself apologizing to the other person. If you need to explain why you reacted the way you did to something, then explain that, too. Then close your eyes, breathe deeply, forgive yourself and let it go.

3. The next step is tougher. Now, meet with (or phone) the person with whom you had the disagreement. Apologize and explain whatever feelings you are having. The person may or may not accept your apology. However, you must forgive yourself.

Rewriting Your Life Script

There are probably many reasons why you react the way you do under certain circumstances. Much of it has to do with your upbringing and childhood conditioning. How you feel about situations and how you live your life was ingrained in you during your early years; it is a big part of how your react now.

There were undoubtedly hurtful, angry and inappropriate comments made to you during childhood. You may have felt abandoned emotionally (or physically) by your mother or father, physically abused, or made to feel inferior to others. You reacted a certain way as a child (silent treatment, explosive anger, low self-esteem) and some of these emotions may surface when you are in a particular situation during adulthood that brings back childhood emotions. Whoever hurt you as a child must be forgiven in your heart. You are an adult now and in control of your emotions and life. No one can hurt you now without your permission.

Exercise

1. Make a list of the most hurtful things that have been said to you.

   - _____
   - _____
   - _____

2. Now, list who said each thing, your age at the time, where you were, and how you felt after each incident. Be specific about how you felt. Did you feel unworthy, unappreciated, angry?

Age	Incident	Feelings

3. Try very had to remember as much as you can about the other person involved. Envision his/her face. Were they screaming or speaking through clenched teeth? Relive the event, and respond in a way that makes you feel good, but at the same time, do not attack the other person.

4. Make a list of the most hurtful things you remember saying to others. Now, write beside each item who the person was, what was happening in your life at the time, and how you felt. (This may be a childhood or adult situation.)

What I Said	To Whom	Why

5. Try very hard to remember as much as you can about the event. Were you screaming or pointing your finger; was the other person in shock or in tears. This time, respond in a way that is not mean or hurtful to the other person, but let him/her know exactly how you are feeling. (With your eyes closed, envision the positive outcome from sharing assertive feelings that were not cruel or hateful.) Envision yourself stepping off an emotional roller coaster.

Communicate, Communicate and Then Communicate More

Every relationship, whether you deal with a person only minutes at a time, or if it is very personal and significant, requires that you communicate with this person so that the relationship is positive. Real communication with another person requires give and take from both people. Just as you want the opportunity to express yourself clearly and completely, you must be willing to give the other person the same opportunity. That requires listening with more than just your ears; this is when you need to learn and use the art of **emotional listening**. When you listen emotionally, you actually listen with your ears, eyes, heart and mind. Put yourself in this person's place and feel what they are feeling. This is also called **empathetic listening.**

Exercise
A Good Listener: List below what you consider to be good listening skills. Check off those skills that you possess.

Good Listening Skills	I Have These Skills

Review the list and consider any areas where you need to improve. The next time you are in an emotional conversation with another person, do everything in your power to really listen and **deep sense** why they are upset. The very words "I understand" can truly calm another human being very quickly.

Reality Check

Remember, you are in control of your emotions, and ultimately your happiness. Perhaps some of your problems would be easier to recognize and work through if you did a thorough assessment or 'reality check' of the root causes. It is very important for you to stay close and in tune with who you are.

One thing you may want to try is to keep a journal and just write down whatever emotions you are experiencing. It is especially important that you write about joyful, celebratory times, just as you write about any pent-up frustrations that you have not verbalized. Keeping a journal will allow you to get things off your chest, and can be an effective tool in helping you work through some issues – whether you are able to solve a problem yourself, or if you decide you want to seek advice or counsel from someone else.

Exercise
1. List 5 things that have made you happy and excited in the past six months. Now list in detail exactly what happened, who else was involved, and what you did or said to ensure that you and others were happy and at peace.

2. Think back and try to remember what feelings you were experiencing during these happy times, and note specifically what you were thinking and what role you played during these events.

3. Make a list of all you can possibly do to ensure you have more joyous times. Be very specific when listing what you will do to make this happen.

4. List 5 things that have made you very sad and/or upset in the past six months. Now, list in detail exactly what happened during those times, who else was involved, and how you reacted to each event.

5. Under each item, note if you think you reacted appropriately; if not, how would you change things now?

6. If you believe that your actions were inappropriate and the feelings you experienced were unavoidable, what do you think you could have done to lessen the sadness and hurt for you, and maybe someone else?

Staying happy and content really are attainable goals. Once you get a true understanding and an appreciation for who you are emotionally, then you will know what makes you happy and can work toward that end. Amazingly, when you are happy with yourself, you will have an uncanny ability to make others happy and at peace when they are in your presence.

Recommended Reading

Principle-Centered Leadership by Stephen R. Covey

Change Your Thoughts – Change Your Life by Dr. Wayne W. Dyer

Twenty-Five Words – How the Serenity Prayer Can Save Your Life by Barb Rogers

Notes:

ABOUT THE AUTHOR

Brenda McDowell-Holmes

Brenda McDowell-Holmes is Founder, President and Chief Executive Officer of McDowell-Holmes & Associates, Inc. The company was established in 2005 to provide personal and professional development services for youth, school districts, business professionals and organizations of all sizes.

McDowell-Holmes & Associates has successfully mentored and counseled youth to overcome obstacles to fulfilling their life purpose. Youth development sessions include Save Our Youth, Stress Management for Youth and Leadership Development. The company also conducts personal and professional development seminars on various topics, including marketing strategies for consultants, women's issues, diversity, wellness and branding and image projection.

Ms. McDowell-Holmes is a veteran of diversified experience in the corporate environment. She is certified in Diversity, Professional Speaking, Customer Service and Youth Issues. She holds a Masters Degree in Business Administration/Human Resources and a Bachelors Degree in Business Administration/Management. Ms. McDowell-Holmes is also a member of several professional organizations, such as Professional Woman Network (Advisory Board), American Business Women's Association, National Association for Female Executives and National Black MBA Association and Toastmasters International. She is also a Real Estate investor.

Ms. McDowell-Holmes is the co-author of several soon to be released books: *You're on Stage: Image, Etiquette, Branding & Style, A Women's Guide for Overcoming Obstacles, Transition & Change, Women s Leaders: Strategies for Empowerment & Communication,* and *Beyond the Body: Developing Inner Beauty.*

She dedicates this book project to her wonderful father and her beautiful mother and angel. I truly believe in angels. She wishes to acknowledge her husband, Willie Holmes, her father Mr. Abraham McDowell, her godmother, Carolyn Crawford Randall, her sisters, brothers, nieces, nephews, and closest friends who believe in her.

"Thank you daddy for believing in me and now I can help motivate people to change their lives. "

Ms. McDowell-Holmes is available to conduct seminars and workshops on a local, national and international basis.

Contact:
McDowell-Holmes & Associates, Inc.
P.O. Box 1583
Stockbridge, Ga. 30281
(404) 663-2418
brholmes@bellsouth.net
www.protrain.net

TWENTY-FOUR

LIVING YOUR DREAMS

By Brenda J. McDowell-Holmes

A dream is a wish your heart makes when you're fast asleep.
In dreams you will lose your heartache -
Whatever you wish for you keep.
Have faith in your dreams and someday
Your rainbow will come shining through.
No matter how your heart is grieving . . .If you keep on believing,
The dream that you wish will come true.
A Dream Is a Wish Your Heart Makes
from the Disney movie Cinderella

Dream Origins
Where do dreams come from? According to the quote above, "A dream is a wish your heart makes." I really believe that this is true. While ideas for dreams may come from different places at different times, unless what you are seeing or hearing resonates with something

deep inside your mind or soul, then these things will not become your own personal objectives in life. In order to be receptive to discovering what your dreams really are, you should stay in tune with not only your innermost thoughts and feelings, but also what your gut and your heart are telling you.

Many times dreams come to us when we are sleeping. Often, our dreams are indicators of our subconscious mind working on something. Sometimes our dreams are boring and lifelike. In fact, it is not unusual for us to dream about a new job or something else we are trying to learn. (This type of dream reminds us that our subconscious is hard at work trying to help us learn something we need to know.) At other times, our dreams are wild. We could be flying or falling, we say and do bizarre things, and there doesn't seem to be any rhyme or reason to the colorful sounds and sensations of this bizarre, unreal world. However, you can be sure that these dreams are important, because they are also a form of our subconscious mind working for us. While we may not understand what they mean, our dreams are important, and if we take the time to try to understand them, we may just find that they hold the key to our heart's desire.

Exercise 1 – Dream Journal
Keep a notebook close to your bed. When you wake up and remember your dream, write it down. After a period of about a month, read over your entries to determine if you can find a pattern. Then, go to the library and check out some books on the topic of interpreting your dreams. See if your dreams fit into one of the patterns or categories discussed in those books. By better understanding the meaning of your dreams, you will have greater discernment into your thought processes.

Dream Squashers

Cinderella had a dream. She wanted to marry a prince. Whether you think her dream was worthwhile doesn't matter, because it was her dream, not yours. One of the problems with dreams occurs when you start to question their validity, because you're listening to people who tell you that your dreams are not feasible. I call these people "dream squashers." It's very important to make sure you surround yourself with people who are dream supporters, rather than "dream squashers. You can easily recognize these people because they are the ones giving you all the practical reasons why something won't work. They'll say such expressions as:

- "If you start your own business, you won't have any steady income, and you won't know how much money you're going to make from month to month. What are you going to do if you can't pay your bills?"

- "Art history isn't a practical major. You need to choose a course of study that will give you a chance of getting a job after you graduate."

- "Acting is such a competitive field. I just don't want to see you get hurt." (In other words, they don't think you have the talent to make it as a professional actor or actress.)

The biggest problem with "dream squashers" is that their arguments make sense. Many times the people who are providing this advice are people who truly care about you. You need to understand that usually one or two events have occurred with dream squashers. Either they had a dream that didn't work out (and they don't want you to get hurt like they did), or they never had a dream in the first place. They can't really understand why you want to take such a big risk, instead of just going down the safe, secure, guaranteed path. What they don't consider is that there is really no safe path in life. There is no such thing as a guaranteed job, secure relationship, or safe road. So, once you understand the underlying motivation for why dream squashers say what they do, it's much easier to ignore them.

You also have to consider that there are a few dream squashers out there who don't really have your best interest at heart. Cinderella's dream squashers were her evil stepmother and two stepsisters, and they were motivated by jealousy and fear. They were jealous of Cinderella's great beauty, and they were afraid that she might actually achieve her dream of marrying the prince. So, they tried to suppress her by keeping her so busy that she didn't have either the energy or the opportunity to pursue her dream. This is also a very real danger for people desiring to live their dreams. They spend their time on areas of their lives that are perhaps necessary, but not really conducive to getting what they really want out of life. Cinderella's stepmother and stepsisters really piled the chores on her. They also tried to hide her beauty by dressing her in rags. What they didn't realize is that you can't hide internal beauty. It shines through, no matter what your appearance.

Probably everyone has had the experience of meeting someone who, on first glance, seemed quite attractive. Then, once you got to really know this person, you realized that, because of his/her negative character traits, in reality this person wasn't good looking at all. (It also works the other way. Sometimes you meet someone who you don't think twice about, but once you get to know this person, you realize that he/she is really beautiful or handsome because of his/her inner spirit.)

Exercise 2 – Your Dream Squashers
Answer the following questions to identify the people in your life who may be squashing your dreams, and then analyze the effect these people are having on you:

1. Who are the people in your life who are your dream squashers?

2. What are some of the things they tell you?

3. Do you buy into what they are saying? Why, or why not?

4. What do you think their motivations are for their discouragement?

5. What can you do in the future to minimize their negative energy and/or lessen its impact on you?

Dreams = Happiness

The reason it's important to ignore "dream squashers" is that they are also, in essence, "happiness stealers." Dreams are the things that give us hope in life. When dreams come true, we experience a great sense of accomplishment, as well as feeling of great joy. Without dreams, there would be nothing to strive for, nothing to look forward to, and no reason to get up in the morning. Dreams give our lives purpose. There is no greater feeling than knowing that we have dreams that we can work to attain; it's what energizes our minds, bodies, and souls. Dreams are what make life worth living.

Dreams are vital to our well being, so it is important to be enthusiastic about accomplishing them. Let's get started with a few steps you can take to start living your dreams.

Exercise 3

Answer the following questions in order to identify you dreams and develop a game plan which you can follow to accomplish them.

1. What are your dreams?

- _____
- _____
- _____

2. What is holding you back from pursuing your dreams?

- _____
- _____
- _____

3. Write out a strategic plan to follow.

- _____
- _____
- _____

4. Determine the first step you need to take, and give yourself a timeframe for completing it.

_____ completion date: _____

Take one step at a time and think positively about your progress.

Invest in your Dreams

Dreams aren't usually easy to achieve. Dreams require us to invest a great deal of ourselves (our time, energy, and yes, sometimes even our money) into doing what is necessary to make our dream a reality. You need to consider any sacrifices you make as an investment in both your future and your happiness.

So, how important is it for you to invest in yourself? Just consider what would happen to a savings account if all you did was put in a lump sum in the beginning (the idea behind your dream), and then you just let it sit there. You might earn a little interest on it if you are lucky, but in the end you'll have more taken out in taxes than you invested in the first place. (This comes in the form of discouragement and the ultimate abandonment of your dream.) On the other hand, if you keep putting money in your account (the time and effort you spend working on your dream), little by little your account will grow until you finally have enough money to retire comfortably (symbolizing the ultimate attainment of your dream).

One of the ways you can invest in your dream is by using your internal power of positive thinking. **You have to really believe in your dreams**. It helps to visualize yourself already having or doing what it is that you want. You can leave no room for doubt. That's why it's vitally important to ignore or stay away from the people who might say or do things that would discourage you from pursuing your dream. In order to live your dream, you must think positively about yourself and your abilities. It all starts inside of you. If you don't believe in yourself, who will? Maybe your family or friends, but that isn't going to be enough. You have to have the internal fortitude to deal with the obstacles that will inevitably occur in the pursuit of your goals. Sometimes we can be our own worst critics in life, and while it is important to understand our faults and weaknesses so that we can try to compensate for them, it is even more important to silence any doubts about whether we can achieve our dreams.

What you need to realize is that you already possess all the talents and passions you need to bring your dreams to light. Also, it is crucial to realize that you are never too old to start living your dreams. Grandma

Moses, one of America's first famous primitive artists, didn't even start painting until she was 75-years-old, and the reason she painted was because her arthritis prevented her from doing needlepoint anymore. You need to realize that the only limitations you will have on your dreams are the ones *you* put on them.

Dream Time

Some dreams come true rather quickly, while other dreams may take a much longer time to accomplish. Have you ever noticed how some people seem to have everything their heart's desire, while other people may wait for a lifetime to achieve just one thing they wanted? While we may not be able to control the time it takes to see our dreams to fruition, we can be persistent and continue to work towards achieving our dreams. Never give up on what you really want in life. It takes courage to live your dream. In my own life, some of my dreams have not happened as quickly as I wanted them to, but I kept on striving in the direction I needed to go to make them a reality. In fact, I am still working on a couple of my dreams, trusting that they will materialize in their own good time. All in all, I am living most of my dreams, and I believe the best is yet to come.

You also need to remember that the path to achieving your dream is not always a straight one. Sometimes things will be going well on your journey, and other times you will encounter difficulties. There are pros and cons for every situation. You just need to realize that problems can make you stronger, because they are always learning experiences. What we sometimes don't see is that there are forces greater than we are that have a bigger and better vision for our dream than we can ever imagine. So, we should always analyze a problematic situation to determine if it is wise to wait for life to get better before moving ahead. (I believe people that I have worked with for years thought that I was really waiting for something better to happen on the job, but in reality, I was waiting for some other situations to clear up in my life that ultimately made me stronger for new work challenges in my life. When I realized that it was time for me take action, I become more serious about my career.) You need to realize that if you are waiting for everything to be perfect, then it's never going to happen. There is never a perfect time. You just have to follow your heart, do what need to do, and be brave in the face of adversity.

Dream Action

One way you can severely limit the chances of accomplishing your dreams is to never take any action toward making them a reality. If you only talk about your dream, but never do anything constructive to make it a reality, you're not really living your dream; you're just dreaming your dream. In order to really live your dream, you have to take action. You should be aware that something very interesting happens when you take concrete steps to fulfilling your heart's desire. You will find that the universe will give you exactly what you need when you need it. That might mean putting the right person in your path to help you, or it might mean getting some unexpected revenue so you can purchase needed items to continue along your dream path.

You also need to be aware that sometimes living your dreams may require you to make some changes in your life that may affect people who are close to you. For example, living your dream may require you to move to another state with a different climate than the one you are used to experiencing. While your family may want to live in the

South, your dream of working in a certain career field may necessitate a move to a colder climate, taking you away from your closest friends. I remember a time when I asked both my husband and my father how they would feel about me accepting a position in a state other than Georgia. While my husband was more than willing to make the move with me, my father had a difficult time with the idea that I would no longer be living within a thirty mile radius of him. Since I had lived in the same area all my life, I had strong family ties and many dear friends in that vicinity. Luckily for me, I had surrounded myself with supportive people, and once my dad realized that moving could bring me closer to my dreams, he reconciled himself to the thought of me moving. When he asked me, "Will you come home about once a month?" I answered yes, knowing that he was now okay with the idea. I also reminded him of the unconditional love that I felt for him, and that nothing in this world would change the deep feelings I have for him.

Have Faith

According to the Cinderella song mentioned at the beginning of this chapter, "Have faith in your dreams, and one day your rainbow will come shining through." Believing in yourself is crucial to obtaining your dream. You have to be confident enough to take some chances, and to believe that your circumstances will improve when you make a real effort to make them better. You just have to start where you are right now, at this moment in time. When you believe in yourself, you recognize something beautiful inside of you is about to blossom. Ruby Ashley, a very close friend of mine, would always tell me: "Believe and you can Achieve." I remember her emphasizing this to me. Her words helped me realize that my dreams are going to manifest, as long as I continue to believe in them. You, too, can be a dream maker. You can also help others make their dream come true by supporting them in their dream quests through your positive feedback.

Dream every day. Do your best to work toward your dreams, regardless of what other people say. Living your dream may require your inner strength, but you need to do whatever it takes to make your dream a reality. Over the years, I have learned to never give up on a dream. However, there were times when I had to change my plan to create a better, more efficient plan. Dreams can and will change over a period of time. Therefore, continue to ask yourself, "What is my dream today?" Stay alert and keep hope alive. Can you see yourself living your dream? As long as you can imagine it, as long as you see it, then it can happen for you. Get prepared for the dream before it happens. Dream big!

I BELIEVE

I Believe there are talents and gifts inside of me.
I Believe I can transform my obstacles and challenges into victory.
I Believe if my goals are going to be, it's up to me.
I Believe in this world, I am destined to make a difference.
I know I am going to achieve, because I believe.
And now, I must proceed.
—Ruby Ashley

ABOUT THE AUTHOR

DOROTHY "DOT" EVERHART, L.S.W.

Dot Everhart is a licensed social worker, currently working as a medical social worker in hospice for Odyssey Health Care in Camp Hill, PA. She has over thirty years of experience working in and with governmental and private social services, as well as churches and religious organizations. Dot's work includes direct casework, counseling, personal life coaching, supervisory and management experience in child welfare, mental health, mental retardation, and drug and alcohol services, as well as pastoral ministry (1976-78) and college teaching (1985-98). She worked in county human services (1978-98) and since 1991 has provided training and consultation in child welfare in Pennsylvania, Ohio, Wisconsin, Indiana, and Minnesota. She writes curricula for training seminars and enjoys creating handouts, presentation visuals and learning activities. Her education includes degrees in elementary education (BA), theology (M. Div.), social work (MSW), and public administration (post-master's certificate).

She is a member of the National Organization for Women, the National Association of Social Workers, the National Association of Female Executives, the Professional Woman Network, and the Unitarian Universalists of the Cumberland Valley. She is also a part-time consultant with The Pampered Chef. She lives in Lemoyne, PA with her life partner of 30 years and her Shih Tzu dog. In her "spare" time, Dot enjoys photography, travel, classical music, cooking (and eating!) and public speaking.

Contact:
Life Compass Coaching
(717) 991-3539
doteverhart@yahoo.com
www.lifecompasscoaching.com

TWENTY-FIVE

DEALING WITH SADNESS AND GRIEF

By Dorothy E. Everhart, L.S.W.

Having an accurate understanding of grief can facilitate moving through its various phases in a healthy and helpful manner, emerging on the other side of grief in a place of adjustment and recovery. Misunderstanding grief can cause us to get lost in it, or to get stuck in one of its phases, delaying the return to our emotional equilibrium, or preventing recovery altogether.

Grief is a measure of attachment. We grieve the loss of people and things to which we are attached. If we do not love, we do not grieve. To the depth or degree that we love and form strong emotional attachments, we experience grief and sadness. While we may attempt to describe our grief altruistically as being in honor of the lost or departed loved one, our grief is more honestly *self*-centered. We grieve *our* loss. We are sad because we feel we have been "abandoned" by the one who left us – through death, separation, broken relationship, or a change in circumstances, such as moving away.

An acrostic of the word "grief" can organize some useful information about the grieving process, which might foster healthy grieving and emotional recovery after a significant loss:

Grief is Good
Recognizable Patterns
Individual Choices
Effective Strategies
Find What Works for YOU!

Grief is Good

Grief is **good**; it is normal. In fact, it is necessary as a healthy emotional process to assist us in working through an emotional loss—whether that loss is of a relationship with a person through death, divorce, or dissolution of a relationship—or whether that loss is of a prized object or possession, such as a car through an accident, or a home through a fire or flood—or whether that loss is of an important status one used to hold in a family or community, such as loss of a job through lay-off or getting fired, or through retirement from a career. Status losses might also be experienced through major life passages, such as "the empty nest" that occurs when children leave home for marriage, careers or education. They might also be felt during seemingly smaller transitions at the end of a term of office in a club or elected community position, or change in job responsibilities at work due to reorganization.

"Normal" grief reactions can include a whole list of emotional, physical, and behavioral reactions. Some of these are: sadness, crying, anger, guilt, anxiety, fatigue, loss of appetite, inability to sleep, forgetfulness, social withdrawal, apathy, emotional or physical numbness, repeated sighing, seeing visions (often of the departed) or hearing voices (often of the deceased), dreams (often of the deceased), a sense of relief (especially after a long, painful illness or in conflicted relationships), preoccupations or "getting stuck" saying the same thing over and over again, feeling helpless about making decisions or completing tasks, and feeling overwhelmed. This is not an exhaustive list, but indicates how widely varied a "normal" reaction might be.

When the grieving person is a member of a cultural group that is different from ours, whether ethnically, religiously, racially, or socially, we need to be aware of how cultural differences might impact their grieving, and learn as much as we can about what is "normal" in their culture, rather than superimposing our cultural expectations on those who do not share our cultural norms and values. For example, in some Caribbean, Hispanic, and African cultures, it is very typical for those who are grieving, especially older women, to see visions or hear voices of the departed one. This might frighten some of us, or we may see it as a sign of mental illness and respond in a manner that will not be helpful or respectful to the grieving person.

Attempting to avoid, deny, or rush grief is unhealthy emotionally, and can lead to dangerous emotional consequences. Sometimes, the professionals we turn to for assistance with grief mislead us, and might even harm us by telling us to "get over it" or to "move on" or to "be done with this", when we are still feeling the loss so intensely that we can't function effectively in our normal routine. A therapist who works in a rural mental health clinic reports that one of her patients told her that the new psychiatrist (after speaking to the patient for only ten minutes during a medication check-up) admonished her that it was time for her to be over her grief of losing her son through a tragic car accident. This was only three days after his funeral!

Some grief experts tell us that it will typically take at least a full year to work through a significant loss; others report that in some situations of traumatic losses, the recovery process can take years—and sometimes even the rest of our lives. When the loss occurs traumatically, such as catastrophic losses in war or terrorist attacks, in murders, in multiple numbers of friends and family in a compressed timeframe, our grief might be complicated by more serious and long-lasting emotional and physical disruptions. We might become clinically depressed, and need medication and therapeutic intervention to help us to manage and recover. We might develop eating or sleep disorders and need professional help, including medications, to return to the healthier patterns that sustained us prior to the loss. We might lose some functional capacities of thinking, concentrating, or decision-making. Some grief-stricken people experiencing complicated grief report feeling so hopeless and powerless that they feel emotionally paralyzed, and unable to complete even the smallest tasks of self-care, like bathing and dressing. Others experience hopelessness at such a level as to contemplate or attempt suicide. Some turn their anger about the traumatic loss outward and attempt or complete acts of revenge, which can complicate their lives and grieving even further. When traumatic losses occur, such as the attacks on September 11th, 2001 or in acts of violence in schools or natural disasters where whole communities are affected, professional support is often made available for anyone who needs it. But, when the trauma occurs to an individual or a family, we might neglect to arrange for similar professional assistance, which might be required because of the extenuating circumstances.

Recognizable Patterns

Grieving has **recognizable** stages and patterns. Perhaps the most famous discourse on grief was written in 1969 by Dr. Elisabeth Kübler-Ross, in her seminal book, *On Death and Dying*. She noted that most of her patients went through five predictable stages after learning that their deaths were imminent. The stages she noted included:

1. Denial
2. Anger
3. Bargaining
4. Depression
5. Acceptance

Some people report experiencing these stages in a different order, or simultaneously with each other. Several researchers believe that we pass through these five stages *before* we actually begin our grief work—and that they are more accurately seen as the stages of our reaction to getting the news about an impending loss, or about the loss just happening.

Before Kübler-Ross' work, there was a four-stage theory of grief, which included these stages:

1. Shock-numbness
2. Yearning-searching
3. Disorganization-despair
4. Reorganization

Others have expanded these four stages into six: loss, protest, search, despair, reorganization, and reinvestment. Some have suggested that the shock of learning of a death or **loss** often prompts us to feel numbness, and to want to pretend that the event didn't really happen, leading to a sense of denial. When we begin to accept the truth of the loss, we **protest** this intrusion of pain in our lives, and rebel against it by expressing anger, confusion and guilt. Sometimes our bodies experience these through physical symptoms of pain or digestive upsets. We yearn for the return of the loved one, and sometimes **search** for their face in a crowd, or think we hear their laughter or their voice, only to be disappointed when we realize that was like a mirage. Some grieving people sit and listen to recorded voicemails over and over again—sometimes taking comfort in hearing the voice, other times torturing themselves with every repetition. Some grieving people take pleasure in smelling the body odor, cologne or aftershave left on clothing that was worn and not laundered. Others will spray the aftershave or cologne on bed sheets or pillows to create an illusion that they are still present. All of these are signs of yearning and searching. Once the reality of the loss sinks in, **despair** may set in. We can no longer fool ourselves into believing that the departed one will return or that he/she is somehow still present through the faint familiar scent. This deepening acceptance of the loss may lead to further expressions of anger, to soul-felt anguish, despair and depression. We are painfully aware of missing the loved one; we feel bereft without them and may feel that our life has lost its meaning and purpose. Then, as time passes, we begin to **reorganize** our lives to accommodate living without them. This may prompt feelings of fatigue from the additional physical and emotional demands of incorporating their chores into our own to-do lists. On the contrary, we might feel some renewed bursts of energy as we learn new skills or relearn less-used ones. Our new identity begins to take shape, and we discover a sense of **reinvestment** in life, with a new sense of self-identity.

Similarly, J. William Worden, in *Grief Counseling and Grief Therapy: A Handbook for the Mental Health Professional (3rd Edition, 2001)* identifies four tasks that a mourning person must complete to successfully mourn the loss of a loved one. These are:

1. To accept the reality of the loss

2. To walk through the pain of grief

3. To adjust to the environment where the deceased is missing

4. To emotionally "relocate" the deceased

Some people emotionally relocate the deceased as "being in heaven" or "becoming an angel" or "lying embalmed in the grave awaiting the resurrection." How someone relocates a loved one will often depend upon their religious belief system, and their unique way within that system of speaking about death and dying. Some have cremains (cremated remains) in an urn on the mantle (or in the closet). Others create an altar in the home or garden in memory of the departed, and go there to spend time together, while others go to the cemetery and place flowers or tokens on the gravesite.

However you observe others and yourself experiencing grief, you will likely see that not every loss is experienced in the same way, and that not all mourners display behaviors or talk about experiencing all of these stages in exactly this order. Some might skip a stage, others might reverse some of the sequences, and still others may feel that they are adding other stages. In any event, you are likely to see that there are predictable, yet not prescriptive, patterns to the way we grieve and mourn. Knowing the stages and patterns can assist us in identifying when someone is grieving "normally", and when their grief might have become complicated or "stuck" because of individual or unique circumstances. It is then that we might assist by suggesting intervention by a professional.

Individual Choices

Each person's way of grieving is unique to him or her. Some of us are very demonstrative in our grief, and others are very quiet and grieve with much reserve. Some of our ways of grieving might have been learned from other family members, and be part of our cultural heritage. Other choices might be unique to us.

News stories show families from the Middle East crying out in wailing tones and throwing themselves over the flag-draped wooden casket as it is carried through the streets of their neighborhood. In other news stories, families sit in darkened rooms in black clothing weeping silently, or looking into the camera with stony expressions. Other funeral processions are entering golden cathedrals with bishops and clergy in robes, and rows and rows of choir members chanting and singing ancient hymns, while using incense and candles. Whichever image is linked to your culture and to your family's way of mourning, it is important to know what your family might expect and choose when you pass—and that their choices and expectations match your own. If not, it is critical that you discuss your wishes well in advance of them having to mark your passing.

Often, families develop traditions and rituals to help them move through a grief experience. Some families have a very precise way of conducting a funeral or memorial service, so it might be a challenge to distinguish one from another. Other families seem to be able to tailor each funeral or memorial to the departed person, choosing flowers, colors, music, poetry, slides and photos that are uniquely reflective of the deceased person's life and loves. Some choose cremation and spreading ashes in gardens or at the beach. Others insist on church services with an open casket viewing, followed by burial in a cemetery and a lunch or dinner back at the church, or in a local restaurant. Which is *correct*? Is there a right or wrong way to grieve and to recognize a loved one's passing?

In *You Only Die Once* (2002), Margie Little Jenkins does a superb job of presenting many options for people to consider concerning end of life issues, and planning for endings and celebrations to mark the passing. She recommends that these discussions and arrangements take place long before anyone receives news of a terminal illness from a physician, or long before there is a knock at the door from the police informing family members of a fatal car accident. She suggests making a special file folder or box to hold all of the instructions and directions about wills, insurance policies, funeral plans, flower preferences, clergy choices, music selections, funeral clothing, casket choices, cremation, etc. She tells about lots of situations where preplanning saved the day, and many situations where no preplanning was done because people refused to talk about death and dying, feeling it is a morbid discussion, and too upsetting. Over and over again, she artfully makes the point that if we have personal preferences about what we want others to do for us at the end of our lives and after we pass, we need to make them expressly known in a way that is recorded clearly and easily accessed by those who will be charged with the responsibility of carrying out our last wishes.

Just as every one of our fingerprints is unique and our life stories are so individual, so also are the ways we may want our lives to be celebrated, to be remembered and memorialized. If we fail to make this clear to our loved ones, we might be left looking on from the other side wishing we had taken the time to express our preferences.

Effective Strategies

There are many, many strategies to use to grieve effectively. Some of us are connected to communities, religious traditions, and family rituals that carry us along through the experience of death and dying and mourning someone's passing. Others of us choose to live outside of these traditions and rituals. We face the challenge of creating or appropriating rituals that will be meaningful for us in doing the work of grief and mourning.

Alan D. Wolfelt, Ph.D. directs the Center for Loss and Life Transition in Fort Collins, Colorado. He discusses grief as a reconciliation process. In one of his books, *The Journey through Grief* (1997), he discusses six "reconciliation needs" that a grieving person must fill in order to "complete" the grieving process. These include:

1. Acknowledging the reality of the loss or death
2. Embracing the pain of the loss
3. Finding ways to remember the person who died
4. Developing a new self-identity without the lost person
5. Searching for (and finding) new meaning to life
6. Receiving ongoing support from others

Here are some suggestions for finding ways to remember the person who died:

- Make a memorial donation in his/her name, perhaps each year on his/her birthday, or at the December holidays.

- Plant a tree or flowering shrub in a garden—your own or in a public garden (with permission) with or without a memorial plaque.

- Donate a book with a memorial inscription to a local library or to a school library, choosing one of their favorite titles, or a book about their hobby or special interest. Consider doing this each year on their birthday, death day, or at another special day—like the first day of fishing season for a person who liked to fish.

- Make a collage of actual pictures or of clipped images from magazines and other print materials that expresses the essence of the departed person's life, and your relationship with them. Place this card in a special place in your home where you will see it, and it can prompt memories about your loved one. The book by Seena B. Frost, *SoulCollage: An Intuitive Collage Process for Individuals and Groups* (2001) gives many helpful hints about how to create such collages, and to use them as part of a visual journal. You will likely find that the gathering of the images and the making of the card will be a healing process in your grief work.

Find What Works for YOU!

Every mourner must find his or her own way through the grief process to emerge healthfully on the other side of the pain of loss. What works for our family members and friends might not work for us. What works for someone from another culture might be something we explore, and find also works for us. What is helpful for a person from another religious tradition is something we try and find helpful for ourselves. We begin to use it, and it becomes our own tradition, whether we practice the religion from which it came, or borrow it and adapt it for ourselves, apart from the religious tradition from which it came.

When we get stuck in our grief or get lost in the process, we need a caring friend to help us find a professional who can assist us in moving through the grief and return to healthful and fulfilled living—ever mindful of our loss, and grateful for the love that passed between us and the one we lost—for without the love and attachment to the one we loved, there would be no need to grieve. Find what works for you and grieve well—whenever you lose what you love. For it is only in grieving well that we become free to love again.

Notes:

THE PROFESSIONAL WOMAN NETWORK
Training and Certification on Women's Issues

Linda Ellis Eastman, President & CEO of The Professional Woman Network, has trained and certified over two thousand individuals to start their own consulting/seminar business. Women from such countries as Brazil, Argentina, the Bahamas, Costa Rica, Bermuda, Nigeria, South Africa, Malaysia, and Mexico have attended trainings.

Topics for certification include:
- Diversity & Multiculturalism
- Women's Issues
- Women: A Journey to Wellness
- Save Our Youth
- Teen Image & Social Etiquette
- Leadership & Empowerment Skills for Youth
- Customer Service & Professionalism
- Marketing a Consulting Practice
- Professional Coaching
- Professional Presentation Skills

If you are interested in learning more about becoming certified or about starting your own consulting/seminar business contact:

The Professional Woman Network
P.O. Box 333
Prospect, KY 40059
(502) 566-9900
lindaeastman@prodigy.net
www.prowoman.net

The Professional Woman Network
Book Series

Becoming the Professional Woman
Customer Service & Professionalism for Women
Self-Esteem & Empowerment for Women
The Young Woman's Guide for Personal Success
The Christian Woman's Guide for Personal Success
Survival Skills for the African-American Woman
Overcoming the SuperWoman Syndrome
You're on Stage! Image, Etiquette, Branding & Style
Women's Journey to Wellness: Mind, Body & Spirit
A Woman's Survival Guide for Obstacles, Transition & Change
Women as Leaders: Strategies for Empowerment & Communication
Beyond the Body! Developing Inner Beauty
The Young Man's Guide for Personal Success

Forthcoming Books:
Emotional Wellness for Women Volume I
Emotional Wellness for Women Volume II
Emotional Wellness for Women Volume III
The Baby Boomer's Handbook for Women

These books will be available from the individual contributors, the publisher (www.pwnbooks.com), Amazon.com, and your local bookstore.